Mary L. Davenport

Primary Speaker for First and Second Grades

Mary L. Davenport

Primary Speaker for First and Second Grades

ISBN/EAN: 9783337779337

Printed in Europe, USA, Canada, Australia, Japan

Cover: Foto ©Thomas Meinert / pixelio.de

More available books at **www.hansebooks.com**

PRIMARY SPEAKER

FOR

FIRST AND SECOND GRADES

COMPILED BY

MARY L. DAVENPORT

TEACHER IN
PRIMARY DEPARTMENT OF MARQUETTE, MICH..
PUBLIC SCHOOLS.

HENRY R. PATTENGILL, Publisher,
LANSING, MICHIGAN,
1892.

PREFACE.

During long service in Primary work, I have felt the need of selections sufficiently short to come within the capabilities of the "Little Ones." This want or need has led to the compilation of such as here are offered to the numerous teachers of that Grade.

Am indebted to "Nursery Publishing Co." and Youth's Companion for many of the poems in the collection. Proper credit is given, when the author is known.

MARY L. DAVENPORT.

"Ever constant, ever true,
  Let the word be—No surrender!
Boldly dare and greatly do,
This shall bring us bravely through;
  No surrender! No surrender!
And though future smiles be few,
Hope is always springing new,
Still inspiring me and you
  With the magic—No surrender!"

PRIMARY SPEAKER.

The School Bell.

Ting—aling—aling
  Goes the great school bell,
Every little boy and girl
  Knows its music well.
"Come right into school!"
  That is what it sings,
Don't you think we should be glad
  When the great bell rings.

Who is He.

There's a little boy you ought to know,
  Who is just as good as good can be,
He always makes a bow—just so!—
  And the folks all say he looks like me.

Truth.

'Tis a little thing to do,
To speak the word that's true,
Yet truth is always best,
And he who speaks is blest.

—*Clark.*

Ding, Dong, Bell.

Ding, dong, bell!
  Brisk and full of cheer,
'Tis the sound we know so well,
  And are so glad to hear.
Ned and Joe and Ruth and Kate
  Run for lunch and book and slate!
They, I'm sure, will not be late!

Ding, dong, bell!
  We shall find today,
More of work we know full well,
  And less of rest and play.
Yes, but think how rich a treat,
  In the class and on the street,
All our dear old friends to meet!
  Ding, dong, bell!

—Eudora S. Bunstead.

A Welcome.

O poor darling papa is out in the storm,
I must hurry and see that his slippers are warm,
And run for his paper and put it down there
Just where he will look for it, close by his chair.
And then I shall sit at the window and wait
And watch, till I see him come in at the gate,
And throw him some kisses—a dozen or more.
They'll do till he gets fairly in at the door.
And then—well! before he can shake off the rain
I shall have every kiss that I gave, back again.
I know he will say as he comes up the street,

"I don't care for rain or for snow or for sleet,
For when I get home I shall certainly see
A dear little girlie there, watching for me."
                                   —*Sydney Dare.*

A Tourist.

Every day away she goes journeying alone,
Just a little baby girl! Isn't fairly grown!
Off she goes without a word—Doesn't take a train,
I can't follow tho' I try with my might and main.
                              —*Youth's Companion.*

Telling Biddy the News.

I've got the best news for you, biddy!
   Stop cackling this minute, and hear,
Our baby has cutted a tooth, biddy,
   The darlingest little dear!
It doesn't show much, but it *feels*, biddy;
   I feeled it three minutes ago.
It's little and shiny and sharp, biddy,
   And 'sides, you know, it'll *grow*.
Oh hum! Seems 'sif I must jump, biddy,
   It's such a beautiful thing!
Le's celebrate—me and you, biddy,
   You cackle, biddy, 'n I'll sing.
There now, I'm better, ain't you, biddy?
   It always helps me to jump.
Same as it does to cry, biddy,
   When your throat's all in a lump.
Now let me look at *your* tooths, biddy,
   Why, there hasn't a single tooth grew!

Aren't you 'shamed as you can be, biddy—
    A great old hen like you?
But may be it's 'cause you *are* old, biddy,
    And I'm sorry as I can be,
We'll go to the tooth-man's, biddy,
    And I'll tell him to put in three.
You're my most intimate friend, biddy,
    That's why I'm so sorry, you see.
But we'll keep it a *secret*, biddy,
    Just only *'tween* you and me.
Say, how does it feel to be old, biddy,
    Without a tooth in your head?
Same as it does to be *young*, biddy,
    'Fore the tooths begin to spread?
But I 'most forgot 'bout the baby,
    Guess I must run and see,
May be another tooth's come, biddy,
O my! who knows but there's *three!*

           —*A. H. Donnell in Youth's Companion.*

In School.

"The word for you today is 'toward,'
I write it here upon the board.
Now try if you with it can make
A sentence clear, without mistake."
Then Teddy's lips pressed tightly down,
His brow was tied up in a frown;
And thought spread over all his face
As dots and crosses found their place.
With capitals and all the rest
He strove to do his very best,
So slowly, carefully he wrote;
"Last night I toward my Sunday coat."

           —*Sydney Dare.*

A Race.

A little tear and a little smile
  Set out to run a race,
We watched them closely all the while,
  Their course was baby's face.
The little tear he got the start;
  We really feared he'd win,   .
He ran so fast, and made a dart
  Straight for her dimpled chin.
But somehow—it was very queer,
  We watched them all the while ·
The little shining, fretful tear,
  Got beaten by the smile.

                          --*Youth s Companion.*

—

What Weather We'll Buy.

We don't want a rainy first of May
  Like the one we had before,
So Teddy and I are going today
  To call at the weather store.
And we'll ask the clerk who is always there
  To show us the very best,
And we'll sort and choose with the greatest care
  Before we dare to invest.

We go so early and play so long
  When we crown our Queen o' the May,
That we want our weather quite new and strong
  And certain to wear all day.
We'd like the kind that is full of sun,
  The same as we had last week
But if there are clouds, why, every one
  Must be warranted not to leak.

                          —*Youth's Companion.*

Planting A Cherry Tree.

Dear little, bright little robins,
With your cosy home in view,
  When my tree has grown
  As big as your own
I'll have this bargain with you:
  If you'll eat the slugs,
  And the worms and the bugs,
You may taste of the cherries, too.

Dear old, fussy old Top-not,
You mustn't scratch there—Shoo! Shoo!
  Now just be good
  And act as you should,
And I'l tell you what I'll do:
  When the tree grows tall,
  The cherries that fall
Shall all be reckoned for you.

Sweet little baby brother,
Dimple and smile and coo,
  For this trim little tree
  I've brought you to see
I planted on purpose for you;
  When you're of a size
  To eat cherry pies,
Why, here will be cherries for you.

—*Youth's Companion.*

Planting Trees.

(FREDDY.)
If we are all to choose and say
What trees we'd like to plant today,
  Seems to me none can be

Half so good as a Christmas tree!
For surely even a baby knows
That's where the nicest candy grows.
 Candy on a Christmas tree!
 That's what pleases me!

(CHARLY.)

Planted out 'twould never bear—
But after all why shoud we care?
 The richest thing is what we bring
 From sugar-maples in the spring.
So now I'll set a maple here,
For feast and frolic every year.
 Sugar from a maple tree!
 That's what pleases me!

(WILLIE.)

Sweets are good most any day,
But as for trees, I'm bound to say,
 A shagbark tall is best of all
 When once the nuts begin to fall.
And so a hickory tree I'll set
And piles of fun and nuts I'll get.
 Nuts from a hickory tree!
 That's what pleases me!

(JOHNNY.)

I shall plant an apple tree,
That's the best of all for me;
 And each kind to suit my mind
 On this one with grafts I'll bind,
Ripe or green, the whole year through,
Pie or dumpling, bake or stew,
 Every way I like 'em best,
 And I'll treat the rest.

—*Youth's Companion.*

Plant Trees.

Plant trees, plant trees, on Arbor Day,
Along the shadeless, dusty way;
Who plants a tree shall surely be
A blessing to humanity.

—Youth's Companion.

Spring is Here.

First cold and then heat;
Gray and gold oft will meet.
First frost and then dew
What is lost buds anew.

First showers and then sun
Bring the flowers one by one.
Birds call full of cheer
Sing they all spring is here.

—Eudora S. Bumstead.

Judy O'Trot.

Pray pause and look
At Judy the cook
Flat in the mud, with grave, wise eyes
She is busy making a batch of pies.

'Tis a dirty place
Just see her face!
But to her the dirt is sugar and spice,
And eggs, and lemons, and all things nice.

And skill is hers!
As she beats and stirs,
To her notion, pies to be perfect must
Have plenty of juice and a frosted crust.

When they are done,
They'll be baked in the sun,
Or she'll make an oven over her hand
By spatting upon it the moistened sand.

Well, well all play
Leads at last in some magical way
Up to the labor real and true
That, in some form or other, all must do.

And so the pies,
Over which now she looks so wise,
May be the very best lesson book
To Judy, the future pastry-cook.

- -*Youth's Companion.*

A Sun Song.

When I hide the people frown;
They all smile when I shine down.
When their world is warm they say,
"Oh, the sun's so hot today!"
While the truth is simply, I
Never change here in the sky.
'Tis their spinning world below
Makes me *seem* to vary so.

—*J. M. L.*

What you keep by you, you may change and mend,
But words once spoken can never be recalled.

—*Roscommon.*

A Puzzled Girl.

Tho' she's small she's not a dunce,
  And she's heard folks say
That the world turns over once
  In a night and day.
Is it all a great mistake?
  She has felt some doubt:
But if she could keep awake,
  She would soon find out.

All her world is flat and round—
  She's right on the top—
May be like a pancake browned,
  It is turned flip, flop!
What a somersault 'twould make,
  How the boys would shout!
Oh, if she could keep awake,
  She would soon find out.

She has vowed that till she knows
  She'll not sleep again;
But her eyelids always close
  Ere the clock strikes ten.
Do the hills and houses shake?
  Are stars tossed about?
Oh, if she could keep awake.
  She would soon find out.

— Youth's Companion.

Katy-Did.

When the evening star comes out
  On the pleasant summer eves,
You can hear the Katy-dids
  Crying out among the leaves,
  Katy did, Katy did,

She didn't, she didn't;
Katy did, yes, she did,
No, she didn't, Katy didn't.

How I wonder what they mean.
In the leaves so thick and green;
What the mischief is that's hid,
Which the little Katy did!
Was Katy once a little girl;
One who did not mind her mother?
Was it known to Katy-dids;
Never known to any other?
Katy did, Katy did,
She didn't, she didn't,
Katy did, yes she did,
No, she didn't, she didn't.
Was she such a naughty child
That, all through the summer mild,
All these insects are forbid
E'er to tell what Katy did?

Oft my darling on the porch,
On each eve when they begin,
Tries, with eager little ears,
Hard to understand their din,
Katy did, Katy did,
She didn't, she didn't,
Katy did, yes she did,
No, she didn't, Katy didn't.
But with all their constant cry
Not my little one or I
E'er can guess the secret hid,
The dreadful thing Katy did.
                    --*Sheldon's Reader.*

To have what we want is riches, but to be able to do without is power.—*Donald Grant.*

Christmas.

1st. Girl—What did I have for Christmas?
      Oh, some bonbonieres and a doll,
A watch, an upright piano,
      And a point lace parasol!
But I wanted a grand piano
      I don't like the tone of this,
And I wanted a diamond necklace—
      Wouldn't that have been bliss?
The bonbons are every one creamy,
      They know I don't like that kind,
And the doll isn't anything extra—
      They said 'twas the best they could find.
Oh, Christmas is always horrid!
      I never get what I expect,
And then I must wait a year longer,
      And again have my hopes wrecked!

2d. Girl—What did I have for Christmas?
      Oh, a Jew's-harp! isn't it sweet?
And this beautiful new china dolly,
      With dress and apron complete!
And I had two sticks of candy,
      Lemon and pepper-mint,
And a splendid long lead pencil,
      And a pretty new dress of print!
Oh, Christmas is always lovely!
      I never expect a thing,
And then I get presents and presents,
      Till I feel as rich as a king!
                —*Youth's Companion.*

Today is yours, tomorrow may not be.

The Merriest Time.

Laugh and be merry, girls and boys,
Over your stockings full of toys!
There is little in life holds half the joys
Of Christmas day in the morning.
                    —*Youth's Companion.*

We Wish You A Merry Christmas.

We wish you a Merry Christmas,
  Our friends and schoolmates all,
Good store of cheer throughout the year
  In cabin, cot, or hall.

We wish you a Merry Christmas—
  Not once, but o'er and o'er—
And at your gate if misery wait,
  Throw open wide the door.

We wish you a Merry Christmas,
  A happy New Year, too;
With vigorous heart to bear a part
  In all you find to do.

A New-fashioned Christmas.

We had been busy talking, for hours, Christmas eve,
Of all the great improvements until—will you believe?—
I felt quite dull and drowsy, and said, 'twixt yawn and sigh,
"Oh! anything old-fashioned had best pass out and die!"

And then I leaned back smiling and quite self-satisfied,
And closed my eye-lids slowly, when, lo! they opened wide
In sheer amaze and wonder, and would you know the cause?
I saw before me standing, the form of Santa Claus.

But, oh! so strange and altered! in clothes of latest style,
And not at all the Santa I'd dreamed of all the while.
But still I recognized him, and said: "I didn't see
You come out from the chimney,—'twas very dull of me."

"The chimney?" said he gruffly, "I beg of you to know
I clamber down no chimneys; I stopped that long ago!"
I said, "Your load was heavy, you're tired; won't you rest?"
"Oh, no," he answered grandly, "my goods were all expressed!"

"You must have found it pleasant—the sleighing, sir, I mean,
The roofs are much more snowy than I have ever seen."
"Indeed!" his air was lofty—"tis not the present mode
To drive a sleigh, I travel by the elevated road."

'Twas all so strange it chilled me, but still I said, "Now, please,
You won't forget to send us one of your Christmas trees?
The children love you dearly and try to be so good."
He said, "No trees hereafter, I'd have it understood.

"In fact, the time is over for Christmas, I should say
Those very old-time customs have really passed away.
We want the very latest, dear madam, you and I,
And, peace, goodwill and Christmas are of a time gone by."

And then he seemed preparing to take his leave and go,
But do you think I let him? I called out bravely, "No!"
I ran to him and begged him, between my sobs and tears,
To leave us blessed Christmas, just as in former years.

To change no little custom; to take no part away;
To leave us dear, old-fashioned, beloved Christmas Day.
And then, just for an instant (my eyes were very dim
With tears), and when I cleared them, I saw a change in him.

His face, 'twas round and jolly, his clothes were as of old.
He had a pack upon his back as full as it could hold.
And as he beamed upon me I heard his reindeer prance,
Then sly old Santa gave me a smile and roguish glance.

"I wish you Merry Christmas!" I thought I heard him say,
And when I tried to answer him, he'd vanished quite away!
But though they say I dreamed it, I know we shall have still
Our dear old-fashioned Christmas, bringing "Peace on earth,
    good-will!"

               Julie M. Lappmann, in St. Nicholas.

Who Is It?

Now, children, there's somebody coming,
   So try to think sharply and well;
And, when I get through my story,
   Just see if his name you can tell.

His hair is as white as a snow-drift;
   But then he is not very old.
His coat is of fur at this season,
   The weather, you know, is so cold.

He'll bring all the children a present
   The rich and, I hope, to the poor,
Some say that he comes down the chimney,
   I think he comes in at the door.

Father Christmas.

Oh, yes, he's certainly been here,
Our own, own Father Christmas dear,
He's filled our stockings to the brim,
And all these presents came from him;
And though we've never seen him yet,
We think he's such a nice old pet.

Christmas Eve.

Dear old Santa Claus, are you there?
  I want to whisper to you;
Jack says you do not care for girls,
  But I'm pretty sure you do.

They say you listen all the time
  To the little girls and boys,
And those who quarrel, scold and fret
  Never get the Christmas toys.

Now, Mr. Santa Claus, forget
  All the naughty things I do,
For oh! such lots and lots of things
  I'm going to ask of you.

I want a doll—a real doll,
  The nicest one in your pack,
With coat, and pants, and cap and all;
  I'm going to call him Jack.

I want a sled to beat the rest
  As we-all slide down the hill,
For Jack will teach me to make it go,
  I am very sure he will.

And I want a pony to ride,
  All summer at grandma's farm;
Jack will go on the old white horse,
  And will keep me safe from harm.
                - *Sheldon's Reader.*

A jolly old fellow, whose hair is so white,
  And whose two bright eyes are blue,
Is making his visits on Christmas night,
  Perhaps he'll call upon you, and you;
  Perhaps he'll call upon you.

The Butterfly.

1st child.—" Pretty painted butterfly,
  What do you do all day?"
2d child.—" 1 roam about the sunny fields,
  And nothing do but play."
1st child.—" Nothing do but play,
  All the livelong day!
 Oh, fie! butterfly,
  To waste your time away."

2d child.—" I see my lovely shining wings
  In every drop of dew;
 And then I think that all the world
  Is looking at them too;
 Looking at them too,
  Yellow, red and blue;
 Then I think that all the world
  Is looking at them too."

1st child.— " Oh, fie! butterfly,
  You vain and silly thing;
 I'd rather be a grasshopper,
  A pretty song to sing.
 I'd rather be the honey-bee,
  That's busy all the day
 Than an idle butterfly
  That wastes her time away,"
     —*Sheldon's Reader.*

Flowers or Weeds.

Cross words are like ugly weeds,
 Pleasant words are like fair flowers;
Let us sow sweet thoughts for seeds,
 In these garden-hearts of ours.
    —*Youth's Companion.*

The First Snow.

O how calm and keen the air!
　O how clear the light!
Grass and weeds and stones are fair
　In their robe of white.
O how bright and strange to view
　Is the land we see!
Snow has made the world anew
　Just for you and me.

All the trees are grand and proud
　In their soft white wool,
With the weight their twigs are bowed,
　They are piled so full.
But they'd be so bare and cold
　If the wind should blow,
Queer old trees to give their gold
　For a coat of snow?

　　　　　　　—*Eudora S. Bunstead.*

On The Farm.

[A toy house, barn, pig, cow, sheep, tree, man and woman; suit motions to words in speaking.]

You see us here upon our farm,
　My tall straight wife and I.
We lead a very quiet life--
　Which no one can deny.

Our pig was never known to grunt,
　Nor yet our cow to moo;
Our sheep has never made a bleat
　We think it strange, don't you?

There's one tree in our orchard; and
  We can not tell the reason,
It never yet has borne us fruit—
  It's always out of season.

Another matter troubles us,
  And sorely hurts our pride:
The man that made our pretty house
  Forgot to make inside.

To paint the house so gay was kind,
  But what a poor inventor,
To make it of a solid block
  Impossible to enter.

And then our barn is quite absurd,
  In height it's not so big
As is our cow; in length its just
  The length of our white pig.

If barn and house were rightly made—
  They're not, oh, what a pity!—
We'd advertise in summer time
  For boarders from the city.
                  —Francis Randall.

Help One Another.

"Help one another," the snow flakes said,
As they cuddled down in their fleecy bed;
"One of us here would not be felt,
One of us here would quickly melt;
But I'll help you, and you help me,
And then what a big white drift we'll see!"
              —G. F. H. in the Parish Visitor.

Soap Bubbles.

Fill the pipe! Gently blow;
Now you'll see the bubbles grow!
Strong at first, then they burst,
Then they go to nothing, oh!

— St. Nicholas.

Lady Golden-Rod.

"O pretty Lady Golden-rod,
  I'm glad you've come to town!
I saw you standing by the gate,
  All in your your yellow gown.
No one was with me, and I thought
  You might be lonely, too;
So I took my card case
  And came to visit you.

"You're fond of company, I know;
  You smile so at the sun,
And when the girls go romping past
  You bow to every one.
How you should ever know them all
  I'm sure I cannot tell;
But when I come again, I hope
  You'll know me just as well.

"I love you Lady Golden-rod;
  You are so bright and fine,
You never have a crumpled frock,
  Or tangled hair like mine.
I think your mamma comes at night,
  When we are all away,
And dresses you in green and gold
  Fresh for another day.

"How tall you are, dear Golden-rod!
    You're taller most than I;
I cannot grow so very fast,
    Although I try and try.
Oh, here's mamma, dear Golden-rod!
    I'll ask her please to stop,
And she shall say which one of us
    Comes highest at the top."

The lovely Lady Golden-rod!
    She surely understood,
For when wee Margie turned around,
    She bent down all she could,
Until the fluffy yellow heads
    Upon a level came,
And Margie's mother smiling said:
    "Your heights are just the same."
                    —*Carrie W. Bronson.*

Getting Acquainted.

"I got acquainted very quick
    With Teddy Brown, when he
Moved in the house across the street,
    The nearest one you see.

"I climbed and sat upon a post
    To look, and so did he;
I stared and stared across at him
    And he stared back at me.

"I s'posed he wanted me to speak,
    I thought I'd try and see—
I said, "Hello," to Teddy Brown
    He said, "Hello," to me."
                    —*Sydney Dare in St. Nicholas.*

Golden-Rod.

Tell me, sunny golden-rod.
  Growing everywhere,
Did fairies come from fairy-land
  And make the dress you wear?

Say, did you get from mines of gold
  Your bright and shining hue?
Or did the baby stars some night
  Fall down and cover you?

Or did the angels flap their wings,
  And drop their glitter down
Upon you, laughing golden-rod,
  Your nodding head to crown?

Or are you clothed in sunshine caught
  From summer's brightest day,
To give again in happy smiles
  To all who pass your way?

I love you laughing golden-rod,
  And I will try, like you,
To fill each day with deeds of cheer—
  Be loving, kind and true.
                    —Our Little Ones.

April.

When April, one day was asked whether
She could make reliable weather,
  She laughed till she cried,
  And said, "Bless you I've tried,
But the things will get mixed together."
                    —St. Nicholas.

Start True.

"Now start me true," cried Fred,
  To his mates on the hill one day,
As he sped on his bright new sled
  From the snowy crest away.
The hill was long and steep,
  While a narrow, shining track
Climbed up through the snowy deep
  To the top of "Camel's Back."

Near by on the mountain side,
  The tallest pine trees grow;
While a dark and angry tide
  Dashes over rocks below.
But Fred, with a steady care,
  Knows well where the dangers lay;
No rock, or a hidden snare,
  Shall turn him out of his way.

How swiftly now does he glide!
  Past gully and stump and curve,
And nothing can turn him aside—
  Not once from the way does he swerve.
"Hurrah!" he cries," "I am there."
  Till the rocks catch up the refrain,
And he waves his cap in the air
  As he touches the snowy plain.

And so, in the journey of life,
  Start true, my dear boys, and pray,
Avoiding intemperance and strife,
  And the evils that lie in the way,
May you thus when eternity's light
  Flashes upon your course at last,
Break forth into songs of delight
  O'er dangers triumphantly passed.
                    —*Mrs. H. C. Blakeslee.*

The Hobby Horse.

[Little boy astride a stick with whip in hand.]

We are off for a canter the school room down,
Past Chalk-box castle and Blackboard town,
Round Rostrum corner and Armchair place,
Then home to the stable at galloping pace.

My horse is a beauty, he goes so fast,
That tables and desks seem flying past,
He never wants whipping, he never kicks,
And he knows me too well, to play any tricks.

Gee up! Ho, Ho! We're off and away,
He's really so frisky I dare not stay,
But I sha'n't tumble off, no, no, not I;
You'll see us come galloping home bye-an-bye.

Birds and Babies.

Birdies with broken wings,
    Hide from each other;
But babies in trouble,
    Can run home to mother.

Bedlam Town.

Do you want to peep into Bedlam Town?
Then come with me as the day swings down
Into his cradle, whose rockers' rim
Some people call the horizon dim.

All the mischief of all the fates
Seems to center in four little pates,
Just an hour before we say:
" It is time for bed now, stop your play."

Oh, the racket and noise and roar,
As they prance like a caravan over the floor,
With never a thought of the head that aches,
And never a heed to the " mercy sakes."

And " pity save us," and " oh, dear, dear,"
That all but the culprits plainly hear.
A monkey, a parrot, a guinea hen,
Warriors, elephants, Indian men,

A salvation army, a grizzly bear,
Are all at once in the nursery there.
And when the clock in the hall strikes seven,
It sounds to us like a voice from heaven.

And each of the boys in a warm night-gown
Marches away out of Bedlam Town.

Ella Wheeler Wilcox.

I'll Put It Off.

Some little folks are apt to say,
    When asked their task to touch,
" I'll put it off, at least today,
    It cannot matter much."

Time is always on the wing,
    You cannot stop its flight;
Then do at once your little task,
    You will happier be at night.

For little duties still put off,
    Will end in " never done,"
And " By-and-by is time enough,"
    Has ruined many a one.

4

Six Years Old.

When Joe, and Kate, and Dick and Bell
  Started to school last fall,
I cried to go, and papa said
  He thought I was too small.

I begged so hard, at last he said,
  "Well, you can go today;
For after this, I'm very sure,
  At home you'll want to stay."

But I'm not tired yet, and you
  Can judge now by my looks,
That though I am but six years old,
  I like my school and books.

A Fairy Shoe.

If you should pick up a fairy's shoe,
You would be lucky the whole year through,
So the folks say; but a shoe so small,
Needs very good eyes to see it at all.

--E. Braine.

Little Midget.

My papa sometimes scolds and says,
  I am always in a fidget;
But mamma says I keep quite still,
  For such a little midget.

My teacher said today, she thought
  That it was very smart
For such a little thing as I
  To learn a speech " by heart."

Ou Grandpa's Knee.

The cosiest place and the snuggest spot,
    In the summer time
    When the days are hot,
And Minnie is tired as tired can be,
Is just to climb up on grandpapa's knee.
        Oh! the dearest place
        To nestle in,
Is on grandpapa's knee, just under his chin.

The Little Dreamer.

A little boy was dreaming,
    Upon his mother's lap
That the pins fell out of all the stars,
    And the stars fell in his cap.

So, when his dream was over,
    What should this little boy do?
Why, he went and looked inside his cap,
    And found it wasn't true.

Throwing Kisses.

Don't think, dear friends, that I'm too small
    To fill a place like this;
I'm big enough to love you all,
    And throw you all a kiss.

A little word, a look, a smile,
    Will never come amiss;
Takes but a moment, as you see,
    To throw you all a kiss.

Dolly's Tea.

My dolly's getting quite grown up,
    She drinks tea every day
Out of wee, blue china cup,
    In quite a lovely way.

I pour it out, because her hand
    Is such a little one
To hold a tea-pot, so I stand
    And serve till tea is done.

And kitty comes, and has her tea,
    We call it that you know,
It's really milk, because you see,
    She likes it better so.

When kitty's done, she always sits
    And washes all her fur;
I don't think many little kits
    Are good and clean, like her.

Dolly can't was her face, and so
    I have to keep her clean;
If she'd been live like pussy—Oh
    What fun it would have been!

                    —E. Braine.

Taking Dolly Out.

[Little girl with doll in her arms.]
I think you must be tired, my dear,
    Of staying in the house,
I'll take you out if you'll be good,
    And quiet as a mouse.

But if you skip and run away,
    And in the meadows roam,
Oh how I shall regret, dear doll,
    You did not stay at home.

Tip-Toe.

[Doll tied to a Christmas tree just beyond reach of little girl standing on tip-toe.]

I'd gladly take you down, my dear,
 The silken sash untie,
If I were a bit taller dear,
 Or you were not so high.

I'm sure you must be tired poor dear,
 Of hanging there all day,
With nobody to speak to, dear,
 And hungry I dare say.

But you're the sweetest thing, my dear,
 On all the Christmas Tree,
And so I can't help thinking, dear,
 You must be meant for me.

Though somewhere I have read, my dears,
 The nicest things hang high,
But may be reached down, my dears,
 If only you will try.
 —*L. Haskell.*

A Poem Postponed.

I want to tell you about my kitten—
 The prettiest kitten that ever purred;
But I've looked my speller through and through,
 And I can't discover a single word
That rhymes with kitten,
Excepting mitten,
 And that is old and too absurd.
So the only thing for me to do
Is just to send you what I've written,
And wait till she grows to be a cat,—
There are ever so many to rhyme with that!
 —*H. C. W. in St. Nicholas.*

What the Daisy Said.

I am a little daisy
  Right from the dewy earth;
I've come to add my sweetness,
  To this bright scene of mirth.

—   ——

When Mamma Was a Little Girl.

When mamma was a little girl
    (Or so they say to me),
She never used to romp and run,
Nor shout and scream with noisy fun,
    Nor climb an apple tree.
She always kept her hair in curl,—
When mamma was a little girl.

When mamma was a little girl
    (It seems to her you see),
She never used to tumble down,
Nor break her doll, nor tear her gown,
    Nor drink her papa's tea.
She learned to knit, plain, seam and purl,—
when mamma was a little girl.

But gradma says,—it must be true,—
    How fast the season's o'er us whirl!
Your mamma, dear, was just like you,
    When she was grandma's little girl.
                    G. F. C.—in St. Nicholas.

Better be small and shine than great and cast a shadow.
                    —*Rev. Theron Brown.*

Little Penelope's Sewing.

Little Penelope took up her needle,
  And tied a knot at the end of her thread;
And when she had found her thimble finger,
  "Now, I must learn to sew," she said.

She sat on the floor and tipped over the basket
  Till she found some pieces, blue, yellow and red;
She cut with her scissors some criss-cross patches,
  "I'll make my dolly a quilt," she said.

She put in her needle, this way and that way,
  She pushed and she pulled till her fingers bled,
And when she had twisted, and puckered and knotted,
  "My doll has a crazy quilt," she said.
                                        —*Anna M. Pratt.*

Who's Afraid in the Dark!

"Not I!" said the owl,
And he gave a great scowl,
And wiped his eye,
And fluffed his jowl
    "Tu whoo!"
Said the dog, "I bark
Out loud in the dark
    Boo-oo!"
Said the cat, "mi-iew!
I'll scratch any who
Dare say that I do
    Feel afraid, mi-iew!"
"Afraid" said the mouse,
"Of the dark in a house?
  Hear me scatter
  Whatever's the matter.
  Squeak!"

Then the toad in his hole,
    And the bug in the ground,
They both shook their heads
    And passed the word round.
And the bird in the tree
The fish and the bee,
They declared all three,
That you never did see
One of *them* afraid
    In the dark!
But the little boy who had gone to bed,
Just raised the bed-clothes and covered his head.
                        —*J. T. in St. Nicholas.*

Spring Time.

A tiny seed am I, in the mold,
Hidden from the great blue sky and the cold.

Now I'll throw a rootlet out, feel around,
There! I've really turned about in the ground!

Did I hear a bluebird sing?   Could it be?
If I did, it must be spring,—I'll go and see.
                        —*F. M. Hill.*

Frowns or Smiles?

Where do they go, I wonder,
    The clouds on a cloudy day,
When the shining son comes peeping out
    And scatters them all away?
I know! -They keep them and cut them down
For cross little girls who want a frown,
Frowns and wrinkles and pouts,—oh, my!
How many 'twould make—one cloudy sky!

I think I should like it better
  A sunshiny day to take
And cut it down for dimples and smiles,—
  What beautiful ones 't would make!
Enough for all the dear little girls
With pretty bright eyes and waving curls,
To drive the scowls and frowns away,
Just like the sun on a cloudy day.
                    —*Sydney Dare.*

The Broken Arm.

Mama, do send for doctor-man,
  And tell him to be spry;
My dolly fell and broke her arm,
  I'm so afraid she'll die.

I thought that she was fast asleep,
  And laid her on the bed;
But down she dropped upon the floor,
  Oh dear! she's almost dead.

Poor dolly she was just as brave,
  And did not cry at all,
Do you suppose she *ever can*
  Get over such a fall?

But when the doctor mends her arm
  And wraps it up so tight,
Then I will be her little nurse,
  And watch with her all night.

And if she only will get well,
  And does not lose her arm,
I'll never let her fall again,
  Nor suffer any harm.
                    —*H. L. Charles.*

5

Santa Claus.

Oh, Santa Claus is a merry prince,
    He rules o'er the Christmas tree!
His castle is built in fairy-land
    On the topmost peak of Glee.

The name of the castle is joyousness,
    And down through its gardens gay
Run Happy river and Merry brook
    To Laughing sea away.

The frisky leaves blow here and there
    In the sweet little dancing breeze,
And fairy birds frolic the livelong day
    Through the beautiful windswept trees.

And here in the gardens are growing the toys
    That ripen for Christmas day,
And our merry Prince has to tell the time
    When they're ready to garner away.

And how, do you ask, does he bring them to earth?
    In a beautiful fairy boat,
That sails along through a white-cloud sea,
    Like a graceful swan afloat.

And when he draws near to the frozen earth,
    He leaps to his loaded sleigh,
He dons his furs and grasps the reins,
    Then, "Hurrah! away, away!"

Now, if you can peep beyond the clouds
    On some wonderful Christmas eve,
I'm sure you will see him sailing down,
    His beautiful gifts to leave.

Children.

What the leaves are to the forest,
  With light and air for food,
'Ere their sweet and tender juices
  Have been hardened into wood.

That to the world are children;
  Through them it feels the glow,
Of a brighter and sunnier climate
  Than reaches the trunks below.

Come to me, O ye children!
  And whisper in my ear
What the birds and the winds are singing
  In your sunny atmosphere.

For what are all our contrivings,
  And the wisdom of our books,
When compared with your caresses,
  And the gladness of your looks?

Ye are better than all the ballads
  That ever were sung or said;
For ye are the *living* poems,
  And all the rest are *dead*.
                —*H. W. Longfellow.*

Beautiful hands are they that do
Work that is earnest and brave and true
Moment by moment the long day through.

A man's manners are his fortune.

A Greeting.

To you our friends, one and all,
I extend a greeting call,
We're glad to see you here
In our school-room dear.

Welcome, welcome, we repeat,
Glad our teacher you to meet,
We will our little pieces say,
In many a sweet and winsome way.

Then, if the time should seem too long
To you, we'll sing a pretty song,
And each home with a happy heart,
Knowing well we did our part
To make the last day remembered alway.

A Letter to Mother Nature.

You dear old mother nature, I am writing you a letter,
To let you know you ought to fix up things a little better,
The best of us will make mistakes—I thought perhaps if I
Should tell you how you might improve, you would be glad
       to try.

I think you have forgotten ma'am, that little girls and boys
Are fond of dolls and tops and sleds and balls and other toys:
Why didn't you--I wonder, now!—just take it in your head
To have such things all growing in a lovely garden bed.

And then I should have planted (if it only had been me)
Some vines with little pickles, and a great big cooky tree;
And trees beside, with gum-drops and caramels and things;
And lemonade should bubble up in all the little springs.

I'd like to have the coasting and the skating in July,
When old Jack Frost would never get a single chance to try
To nip our cheeks and noses; and the Christmas trees should
    stand
By dozens, loaded!–in the woods!–now, wouldn't that be grand?

Ah! what a world it would have been, how could you, madam,
    make
Such lots of bread and butter to so very little cake?
I'd have it just the other way, and every one would see
How very, very, very, very nice my way would be.

But, as I cannot do it, will you think of what I say?
And please, ma'am, do begin and alter things this very day.
And one thing more—on Saturdays don't send us any rain,
Good-by. If I should think of something else, I'll write again,
                      —S. Dare.

The Bunch of Keys.

Hearts like doors, will ope with ease
  To very, very little keys;
And don't forget that they are these:
  "I thank you, sir," and, "If you please."

A Drawing Lesson.

(Suit actions to the words. Drawing done in the air,)
A line going this way, one like it below,
  With two others here and there,
Make the edges and corners,
  Of the figure we call a square.

With the fore-finger now of this right hand of mine
  I go round and round with care;
No corners at all, and only one edge
  Has my circle up in the air.

Watch me again for I'm going to make
A triangle with edges three,
One line at the bottom, two meeting above,
Like toboggan slides—don't you see?

Wonderful Things.

(Suit the actions to the words.)

Oh, my arms are wonderful things!
They can move up and down like wings;
They can go round and round, without any sound;
I can fold them up and straighten them out;
Oh! my arms they are wonderful things!

And my hands are curious too!
And many things they can do;
They can catch and throw, I can clasp them—so!
And double them up into two little fists;
Oh! my hands they are wonderful things!

What can my legs do? let me see!
They can swing from the hip, and bend at the knees;
They help me to step, to hop and to jump;
Oh! my legs they are wonderful things.

What we ought not to do we should never think of doing.

Dare to be brave in the cause of the right;
Dare with the enemy ever to fight.

For Concert Recitation.

We'll all rise up together,
We'll clap our hands together,
    And show you how
    To make a bow;
And all turn round together.

We'll raise our arms together,
We'll let them fall together,
    And show what fun
    It is to drum;
And all sit down together.

We'll fold our arms together,
We'll sit up straight together,
    Good children we
    All mean to be,
Let's sing a song together.
            "Sing Pat-a-cake," etc.

(Words indicate the motions.)

When we see the dishonor of a thing, then it is time to renounce it.—*Plutarch.*

Over and Over Again.

Over and over again,
    No matter which way I turn,
I always find in the book of life
    Some lesson that I must learn;
I must take my turn at the mill,
    I must grind out the golden grain,
I must work at my task with a resolute will
    Over and over again.

We cannot measure the need ·
   Of even the tiniest flower,
Nor check the flow of the golden sands
   That run through a single hour,
But the morning dews must fall,
   And the sun, and the summer rain
Must do their part, and perform it all
   Over and over again.

Over and over again
   The brook through the meadow flows,
And over, and over again
   The tireless mill-wheel goes.
Once doing will not suffice,
   Though doing be not in vain,
And a blessing failing us once or twice,
   May come, if we *try again*.

The Stars and Daisies.

The stars are tiny daisies high;
   Op'ning and shutting in the sky,
While daisies are the stars below,
   Twinkling and sparkling as they grow.

The Doll's School.

The dollies were lonesome one day,
For their mama had gone away,
When the largest of all jumped up on a stool,
And said, " Listen! who wants to play school? "

" I do," "so do I," answered each of the rest.
" Well! I'll be the teacher, if you'll do your best; "
So they stood up before her in a nice little row
With their hands down beside them, looking just so!

"Hark!" said the teacher, "First turn out your toes,"
One man and two men are how many, who knows?"
"I know," said Doll Dimple, "I know, its three men."
"Very good," said the teacher, "Now who will count ten?"

A fat little boy doll spoke out quickly then,
"One, two, three, four, five, six, seven, eight, nine, ten."
"Well done, little boy, do you know you've ten toes?"
But here comes a whisper from dear little Rose.

"I know something better'n all the rest,
This is my right hand and this is my left,"
"Now its my turn," a large wax doll spoke now,
"East and west I can point, north and south I can bow."

"Look," said the teacher, "It's time for good-by,
But before we say it, let's a little song try."

Bunny-Coat.

Little gay Bunny-coat, skipped into bed,
Nothing was seen of him but his gray head.
Where was his bed think you? Where did he dream?
You'll laugh when I tell you, so droll does it seem.
In little Ruth's pocket, in her apron so white,
Little Gray Bunny-coat slept all night.

Winter.

Cold winter is upon us;
    The snow will soon be here,
The leaves are shaken from the trees,
    The days look dark and drear.

The flowers all are resting
    Beneath the frozen ground;
And birds and bees and creeping things
    Seem wrapt in sleep profound.

Yet winter has its pleasures,
  E'en midst its frost and snow,
When quickly o'er the ice-bound pond
  The skaters gladly go.

The cold hard roads are pleasant,
  ‒ On which to walk or run,
And when the snow is piled up high,
  Oh then, don't we have fun?

Yes, though the skies are dreary,
  And fierce the chill winds blow,
We love the hoary winter time,
  And e'en the fair white snow.

Pop Corn.

Oh, the sparkling eyes,
  In a fairy ring!
Ruddy glows the fire,
  And the corn we bring.

Tiny lumps of gold
  One by one we drop;
Give the pan a shake,
  Pip! pop! pop!

Pussy on the mat
  Wonders at the fun;
Merry little feet
  Round the kitchen run.

Smiles and pleasant words
  Never, never stop;
Lift the cover now,
  Pip! pop! pop!

What a pretty change!
　　Where's the yellow gold?
Here are snowy lambs
　　Nestling in the fold.

Some are wide awake,
　　On the floor they hop;
Ring the bell for ten!
　　Pip! pop! pop!
　　　　　　　—*Our Little Ones.*

Dolly's Complaint.

My name is Lady Ethel;
　　How d'ye do? How d'ye do?
My hair is curly yellow,
　　My eyes are glassy blue.

I came with gay old Santa,
　　So my name he should know,
And he called me Lady Ethel
　　Two long, long years ago.

My little mama loved me,
　　From the day that I came,
So I wouldn't mind her spankings,
　　If she wouldn't change my name.

At first she called me Ethel,
　　Then Queen Bess, Rosa Belle,
And Dolly, Polly Adeline,
　　And they did pretty well.

But since her fine French doll came,
　　Oh, I think 'tis so mean!
She sits me in the corner
　　And calls me Evergreen!
　　　　　　—*E. S. C. in Our Little Folks.*

A Little Boy.

If I were a little bird,
  I'd sing my sweetest song;
I'd take a journey to the sky,
  And frolic all day long.

If I were a pussy cat,
  I'd chase the rats and mice,
And have sweet cream for supper,
  And everything that's nice.

If I were a tiny mouse,
  I'd gnaw the soft new cheese;
When Tabby wasn't in the way,
  I'd do just as 1 please.

But I am a little boy
  Just learning what to do;
And every day, it sems to me,
  I find out something new.

I get up in the morning
  And play with Tom and Nell;
But when I am as old as they,
  I'll go to school as well.

I'm very little to be sure,
  But then I'm only four;
And some day I'll be older,
  And know a gread deal more.

                    —*Our Little Ones.*

Kind hearts are the gardens,
  Kind thoughts are the roots,
Kind words are the blossoms,
  Kinds deeds are the fruits.

A Queer Little House.

There's a queer little house and it stands in the sun;
When the good mother calls the children all run,
While under her roof, they are cosy and warm,
Though the cold wind may whistle and bluster and storm.

In the daytime this queer little house moves away,
And the children run after it happy and gay;
But it comes back at night, and the children are fed.
And tucked up to sleep in a warm feather bed.

The story of this funny house is all true;
I have seen it myself, and I think you have too;
You can see it today if you watch the old hen,
When her downy wings cover her chickens again.

The Pansies.

The dear little pansies are lifting their heads,
    All purple and blue and gold,
They are covering with beauty the garden beds,
    And hiding from sight the dark mold.

The dear little pansies they nod and they smile,
    Their faces up-turned to the sky,
" We are trying to make the world pretty and bright,"
    They whispered to each passer by.

Now all little children who try ev'ry day,
    Kind hearted and loving to be,
Are helping the pansies to make the world bright,
    And beautiful; don't you see?

Empty barrels give the most sound.

Little Leaves.

"Come little leaves," said the wind one day,
"Over the meadow with me and play.
Put on your dresses of red and gold,
For the summer is gone and the days grow cold."

Soon as the leaves heard the wind's low call,
Down they came fluttering, one and all.
Over the fields they danced and flew,
Singing the soft little songs they knew.

Dancing and whirling the little leaves went,
Winter had called them and they were content.
Soon fast asleep in their earthly bed,
The snow laid a coverlet o'er their heads.

Jack.

Two pointed ears on a little round head.
  Two eyes very bright and black,
A funny snub nose and a curled up tail,
  That's my little dog Jack!

A shaggy brown coat to keep him warm,
  Four paws to make pretty tracks,
A dear little voice that says "bow-wow,"
  That's my little dog Jack!

Hurrah for the Flag.

There are many flags in many lands,
  There are flags of every hue,
But there is no flag however grand
  Like our own "Red, White and Blue."

I know where the prettiest colors are,
  And I'm sure if I only knew
How to get them here I could make a flag
  Of glorious "Red, White and Blue.

I would cut a piece from an evening sky,
  Where the stars were shining through,
And use it just as it was on high,
  For my stars and field of blue.

Then I'd want a part of a fleecy cloud,
  And some red from a rain-bow bright;
And put them together side by side,
  For my stripes of red and white.

We shall always love the "Stars and Stripes,"
  And we mean to be ever true
To this land of ours and the dear old flag,
  The Red, the White, the Blue.

Then hurrah for the flag! our country's flag,
  It's stripes and white stars too;
There is no flag in any land,
  Like our own "Red, White and Blue!"

The Trout's Sad Fate.

"I'm very tired of little fish!
  I wish a worm I had."
So spake a young and lively trout;
  "To change I should be glad."

"My dear," the mother quickly cried;
  "Don't think of such a thing!
The only worms that come to us
  Are fastened to a string!"

"And something even worse than that,
    Is hidden underneath,
For of a sharp and bitter hook,
    The worm is but the sheath."

But, ah! this naughty little fish,
    Was sure he better knew;
And soon he left his mother's side
    To get a nearer view.

"Its small, but then its very nice,"
    The fisherman did say;
And quickly put another worm,
    Upon his hook that day.

The mother waited long that night,
    And she is waiting still!
O! sad the fate of poor young trout,
    Who had his foolish will.

Grown-up Land.

BOY.

Merry Christmas! fair maid, with the lashes brown,
Can you tell me the way to Womanhood Town?

GIRL.

Oh, this way, that way—never a stop;
'Tis picking up stitches that grandma will drop.
'Tis kissing the baby's troubles away;
'Tis learning that cross words never will pay;
'Tis reading and playing; 'tis saving the cents:
'Tis loving and smiling, forgetting to frown
Oh, that is the way to Womanhood Town.

Just wait, my brave lad, one moment, I pray;
Where is Manhood Town?   Can you tell the way?

BOY.

Oh, by toiling and striving to reach the land,
A bit with the heart, a bit with the hand;
'Tis by climbing up the steep hill, work;
'Tis by keeping out of the wide street, Shirk;
'Tis by always taking the weak one's part;
'Tis by giving mother a happy heart;
'Tis by keeping bad thoughts and actions down—
Oh, that is the way to Manhood Town!

BOTH.

And the lad and the maid ran hand in hand
To their fair estates in the grown-up land.

The Little Maid.

I know a little maiden
Whom I've often seen arrayed in
Silks and satins, but not always:
She's a handsome little elf—
For she always helps her mother:
And her sister and her brother,
And lives for all around her.
Never thinking once of self.
So she laughs and she sings,
And the hours on happy wings
Shower gladness on her pathway as they flee.
Now need I tell you, my darling little friends,
She's as happy as a child can be?
And, surely, she's the little maid for me.

Good breeding is like affection—one cannot have too much
of it.

7

Where Did They Go.

Grandma says we little witches
Make her drop so many stitches.
Laughing till she fairly shakes
At our pranks; but she mistakes—
For when I bought my little basket
(Just myself, she didn't ask it),
To hunt her stitches on the floor,
(A dozen dropped, she said, or more),
There wasn't one, that I could find!
Poor grandma must be getting blind.

S. D.

Beautiful Flakes of Snow.

O beautiful flakes of snow,
    Falling so softly around,
I wonder what good you do,
    By covering all the ground?

"Dear children," the little flakes said,
    "We have our work to do,
By covering the roots and plants,
    We keep them the winter through."

"Ah, no!" the pussies said,
    We couldn't and we wouldn't do that;
We belong to fairy folks,
    And we are their pussy cats.

The years write themselves on human hearts as they do on
trees, in hidden inner circles of growth which no eye can see.

Pussy Willows.

Pretty pussies down by the brook,
　Swinging away to and fro,
On the bending willow boughs,
　Like pussy cats all in a row.

If I put you down by the fire,
　You pussies so cunning and shy,
I wonder if you'll turn
　Into pussy cats by and by?

A Game of Tag.

A grasshopper once had a game of tag,
　With some crickets that lived near by,
When he stubbed his toe and over he went,
　In the twinkling of an eye.

Then the crickets leaned up against a fence,
　And laughed till their sides were sore,
But the grasshopper said, "you are laughing at me
　And I shan't play any more."

So off he went, tho' he wanted to stay,
　For he was not hurt by his fall,
And the gay little crickets went on with the game
　And never missed him at all.

A bright-eyed squirrel called out as he passed,
　Swinging from a tree by his toes,
"What a foolish fellow that grasshopper is,
　Why he's bit off his own little nose."

Naughty Johnny Snarl.

Naughty Johnny Snarl hid himself one day,
In the pretty curls of our darling May,
There he tied hard knots in her lovely hair,
Tangled, pulled and jerked every lock so fair.

But her mamma came with a brush and comb,
Smoothed the curls and drove naughty Johnny home.
Now for other curls Johnny hunts about;
And he'll find yours too—if you don't look out.

Dolly's Lullaby.

Now shut up your eyes little doll,
    And mama will rock you and sing;
So cuddle up close in my arms
    Dear dolly, my beautiful thing.

SINGS.

Now hush-a-by, rock-a-by doll,
    My darling with eyes of deep blue;
You know that there is in my heart,
    The truest of love, dear, for you.

"The Grand Pacific."- Chicago.

'Twas a rather small engraving of a very large hotel
That little Grace was studying so earnestly and well;
And at last she softly murmured,—this funny little mouse,—
"So that big 'normous building is Gran'pa Cific's house!"
"Who are the Cific's, anyway? mamma, I want to know:
I've heard so much about them—I've never seen them, though,
And it's always Grandpa Cific. I think there ought to be
A dear old Gran'ma Cific that I might go and see."

B. Chandler.

A Letter

Dear postman, please bring me a letter,
  From papa who's over the sea,
He sailed away last September,
  It seems most a year to me.

And please sir, I don't care for stories,
  Of the folks who live over the sea,
I want him to hug me in writing,
  And send twenty kisses to me.

But then if you can't bring a letter,
  So many miles over the sea,
Why, mama and I have decided,
  You'd better bring papa to me.
                       A. S. Roe.

      Idleness means failure;
      Work means success.

The Baby's Creed.

I believe in my papa,
  Who loves me—oh, so dearly!
I believe in Santa Claus,
  Who comes to see me yearly.

I believe the birdies talk
  On the boughs together;
I believe the fairies dance
  O'er the fields of heather;

I believe my dolly knows
  Every word that's spoken;
I believe it hurts her, too,
  When her nose is broken.

Oh, I believe in lots of things—
I can't tell all the rest—
But I believe in you, mama,
First and last and best!

Charles. H Lugrin.

Grandma's Angel.

"Mama said: 'Little one, go and see
If grandmother's ready to come to tea.'
I knew I mustn't disturb her, so
I stepped as gently along, tip-toe,
And stood a moment to take a peep—
And there was grandmother fast asleep!

"I knew it was time for her to wake;
I thought I'd give her a little shake,
Or tap at her door or softly call;
But I hadn't the heart for that at all.
She looked so sweet and so quiet there,
Lying back in her high arm chair,
With her dear white hair, and a little smile,
That means she's loving you all the while.

"I didn't make a speck of a noise;
I knew she was dreaming of little boys
And girls who lived with her long ago,
And then went to heaven—she told me so.

"I went up close, and I didn't speak
One word, but I gave her on her cheek
The softest bit of a little kiss,
Just in a whisper, and then said this,
'Grandmother dear it's time for tea.'

"She opened her eyes and looked at me,
And said: 'Why, Pet, I have just now dreamed
Of a little angel who came and seemed
To kiss me lovingly on my face!
She pointed right at the very place!

"I never told her 'twas only me;
I took her hand and we went to tea."
—*Sydney Dare. St. Nicholas.*

Winter.

'Tis snowing fast, hurrah! hurrah!
  Come over the hills away;
Away we'll run for healthy fun.
  And in the snow-drifts play.

Let me but pull my mittens on,
  I'll make the snow-balls fly;
If you look out the window, Nell,
  You'll see them whizzing by.

Papa thinks I'm not old enough
  Just now to learn to skate;
And mother says another year
  Will not be long to wait.

But famous forts I mean to build,
  And on the ice I'll slide;
How swiftly o'er the glassy crust
  I shall securely glide.

Oh, glad am I the frost has come!
  What merry rides we'll take!
We soon shall hear the jingling bells
  Their thrilling music make.

I know that lovely summer brings
Its many fruits and joys;
But then old frosty winter gives
Rare fun to lively boys.

—From the Nursery.

A Young Seamstress.

" I am learning how to sew," said an eager little maid;
"I push the needle in and out, and make the stitches strong;
I'm sewing blocks of patch-work for my dolly's pretty bed,
And mama says the way I work it will not take me long.
Its over and over—do *you* know
How over and over stitches go?

I have begun a handkerchief; mama turned in the edge,
And basted it with a pink thread to show me where to sew.
It has Greenaway children on it stepping staidly by a hedge;
I look at them when I get tired, or the needle pricks, you
know.
And that is the way I learn to hem
With hemming stitches—do *you* know them?

Next I shall learn to run and darn, and back-stitch too, I guess,
It wouldn't take me long, I know, if 'twasn't for the thread;
But the knots keep coming, and besides—I shall have to con-
fess—
Sometimes I slip my thimble off, and use my thumb instead!
When your thred knots, what do *you* do?
And does it all turn brownish, too?

My papa, he's a great big man, as much as six feet high;
He's more than forty, and his hair has gray mixed with the
black;
Well, *he* can't sew! he can't *begin* to sew as well as I.
If he loses off a button, mama has to set it back!
You must not think me proud, you know;
But I am seven, and I can sew!"

—M. S. B. Branch.

The Top Brigade.

Hurrah for spring weather!
  We'll buy some new tops,
And start out together
  With hippity hops.

—R. M.

The little Girl who would not say "O."

A little girl wouldn't say "O,"
(She was learning her letters, you know;)
And the very same night she awoke in a fright,
For the letter-land king on his throne
Said "O" in a thunderous tone,—
And it startled her so that she quickly said "Oh!"
And the little girl's trouble was done.

—M. A. L.

Little Maud's Story.

I'm going to tell you a story—
  It's nice, I know you'll say;
Not an old tale worn out and stale –
  I made it myself, today.

There was once a beautiful princess—
  Oh, ever so long ago!
When fairies and kings and all such things
  Were common enough, you know.

And oh, she was awfully lovely!
  With eyes as blue as the sky;
Slender and fair, with long light hair,
  And about as big as I.

But oh, she was awful unhappy!
   And if ever she smiled at all,
'Twas once in a while, a weak little smile,
   When she played with her Paris doll.

For she had such *terrible* teachers!
   And lessons she could not bear;
And she hated to sew, and she hated—oh,
   She *hated* to comb her hair!

Well, one day, she wandered sadly
   In a dark and dismal dell;
When, do you know, she stubbed her toe,
   And tumbled into a well!

The well was wet and slimy,
   And dark and muddy and deep,
But the frogs below, they pitied her so,
   They scraped the mud in a heap.

And then they clubbed together,
   And a toadstool tall they made;
And safe on that the princess sat,
   And waited for mortal aid.

And she, to keep from crying,
   And her anxious fears disable,
Repeated fast, from first to last,
   Her multiplication table.

And all the songs and verses
   She had ever learned to say,
Books she had read, pieces she'd said,
   And the lessons of yesterday.

Now, a prince there came a riding
   In the forest thereabout;
When he saw the fair maid sitting there,
   Of course he helped her out.

And, of course, they rode together,
Till they reached the palace-gate,
Where they alighted, their tale recited,
And the wedding was held in state.
—*M. M. Gow in St. Nicholas.*

The Birthday.

Perhaps you remember
I came in November,
'Twixt fading of flowers and falling of snow;
I was such a wee baby,
You doubt this, it may be?
But bless you! since then I've done nothing but grow.

But life now looks shady,
For I'm quite a young lady,
And cares keep me busy as bees in a hive;
But please to remember
On the first of November
Kind friends will be welcome and I will be five.
- -*From Inter-Ocean.*

Say.

Say, if you were a mouse,
Would you take any risk with a trap
That goes off with a snap,
For an old bit of cheese?
Or would you go to bed,
With a whole neck and head,
And a hungry pain spoiling your ease?
—*S. B. Ricord.*

Beware.

'Tis only trouble at the last
  That's sure to come from sinning;
If you would shun its bitter end,
  Beware of its beginning.

—*M. D.*

Grandma's Surprise Party.

They all went down the garden-walk,
  And saw the flowers bloom,
Each picked a bunch—a pretty bunch—
  To put in grandma's room.

And grandma will be *so* surprised!
  What can she say or do?
She'll give each girl and boy a kiss,
  And give the baby two.

—*C. J. Taylor in St. Nicholas.*

Maiden-Hair.

" What a beautiful plant!" said little Ned,
  As he touched it with loving care;
" I never have seen it,—please tell me its name,"
  And we answered him; "Maiden-hair."
Ned laughed, as he looked at the pretty fern,
  The name was so funny and new;
Then said, as he looked at the tiny stems;
  "Why, here are the hair-pins too!"

- --*By Bessie Chandler.*

Why?

Why have the bluebirds come with painted wings?
Why is the great earth full of lovely things?
Golden stars in the grass, rosy blooms in the trees,
Wafts of scent and song blown on every breeze?

Why? Do you hear afar the tread of little feet
Touching the golden stars, crushing the clover sweet?
Do you hear soft voices sing: "We have thrown our
        books away!
Dear earth, we come to you for rest and play?"

Well the good earth knows when school is out;
And so she molds the rose and brings the birds about,
She spreads green boughs abroad to shade the way;
And makes her meadows meet for holiday.

—*By Mrs. M. F. Butts.*

Fishing.

By hook and by crook, to bother the cook,
    The little boy catches some fish,
Then home with his brother, to show to his mother,
    O what better fun could he wish?

A Smart Boy.

(Sitting with slate and pencil.)

I'm glad I have a good-sized slate,
With lots of room to calculate,
Bring on your sums! I'm ready now;

My slate is clean; and I know how.
But don't you ask me to *subtract*,
I like to have my slate well packed;
And only two long rows, you know,
Make such a miserable show;
And, please don't bring me sums to *add*;
Well, multiplying's just as bad;
And, say! I'd rather not *divide*—
Bring me something I haven't tried.

———

Youth and Age.

A funny thing I heard today
    I might as well relate,
Our Lil is six, and little May
    Still lacks a month of eight.

And through the open play-room door,
    I heard the elder say;
"Lil run down stairs and get my doll,
    Go quick now,—right away!"

And Lillie said (and I agreed
    That May was hardly fair)
"You might say 'please,' or go yourself—
    I didn't leave it there."

"But, Lillie," urged the elder one,
    "Your little legs, you know,
Are younger than mine are, child,
    And so you *ought* to go.
            —*M. H. F. Lovett, in St Nicholas.*

The work of the world is done by *few*,
God asks that a part be done by *you*.

Little Mischief.

(Little girl with gray felt hat on her head, in which is stuck a long hen's feather.)

Perhaps I *am* little. But what of that?
I am big enough to find Charlie's hat.
He left it here with its queer little feather,
Lying right out in the wind and weather.
He's searching now; I can hear him call;—
Never thinking of me, because I'm small,
He's shouting and calling to this one and that,
"I say, have you seen my gray felt hat?"

Oh, yes, I've seen it! But *he* doesn't know,
He thinks I'm nothing but Baby Bo.
That's what they called me before I could walk;
And now I can run and jump and talk,
See him stooping and hunting out there in the hay!
He'd find it right off, if he'd just look this way.
Why doesn't he see me? Oho! Oho!
He thinks I am nothing but Baby Bo!

Why the Chick Came Out.

Benny Bright-Eyes, climbing over
Heaps of crisp and fragrant clover,
Spies the dearest, cutest thing,
Hiding under biddy's wing.

What sees Benny next? A wonder!
Rudely pushed out from under
Biddy's breast, an egg comes sliding,
In its shell a chicken hiding.

"Ah!" says Benny as he gazes,
And his merry blue eyes raises,
"I know why his house he's spoiled;
He's afraid of being boiled."

—*M. J. Taylor in The Nursery.*

The Dear Little Kitty.

We found this dear little kitty
   Way under the entry floor,
Ned crept through the tiniest opening
   That must be the old cat's door.
And he called me to come and take it,
   'Twas as lovely as it could be,
And it really believes I'm its mother,
   For its eyes are not open to see.

June.

My sister May
Has gone away
   With April and his showers,
I come apace
To take her place,
   Accept my gift of flowers.
                          —*The Nursery.*

Mamie's Lecture.

(Little girl before an open dressing case, holding a hand mirror, and talking to her own face seen in it.)

"Little girl! what are you doing in my papa's dressing-case? Don't you know it's very naughty for little girls to get into dressing cases? Little children should be seen and not heard. I'll go tell my mamma 'bout you—how you went and got into my papa's dressing case. It's no business for little girls. I 'shamed of you."

Watch Your Words.

Keep a watch on your words, my darlings,
  For words are wonderful things;
They are sweet like the bee's fresh honey,
  Like the bees they have terrible stings.

The Mud Pie.

Tell me little housewife,
  Toiling in the sun,
How many minutes
  Till the pie is done?
Johnny builds the oven,
  Katie rolls the crust,
Daisy finds the flour
  All of golden dust.
Turn it so, and roll it so,
  What a dainty size!
All the plums are pebbles,
  Hot mud-pies!

Littles.

Little moments make an hour;
  Little thoughts, a brook;
Little seeds, a tree or flower;
  Water-drops, a book;
Little deeds of faith and love
Make a home for you above.

Roses of the cheek will fade;
  Beauty pass away;
Loving words and gentle deeds
  Never *can* decay.

9

The Lady Girl.

(Little girl with curls; a cap with wide frill; a handkerchief over her shoulders, crosssd in front, sitting with hands crossed in her lap.)

Oh! I'm my mama's lady-girl,
    And I must sit quite still;
It would not do to jump and whirl,
    And get my hair all out of curl
And rumple up my frill.
    No, I'm my mama's lady-girl,
So I must sit quite still.

The Naughty Doll.

(Little girl holding a doll up by the arms.)

Now, dolly, can you look me in the face and say you didn't go down to the river while I was at church? You can't say it, I see you can't, and you must go to bed without your supper.

The Fortune.

(Little girl holding daisy, with leaves previously loosened, blowing off leaves as she recites—throwing it away as she says "I don't care" etc.)

Tell me, daisy, 'ere I go,
Whether my love is true or no,
One leaf off; He loves me, What?
One more leaf and he loves me not,
Three leaves! Will he? Four leaves! So,
He never will love me—oh, no, no!
I don't care what a daisy says!
I'm sure to get married one of these days,

Be ashamed to catch yourself idle.

A Hard Lesson.

(One little girl and two little boys sitting on a bench studying their lesson. A larger girl or boy recites the following.)

One little girl and two little boys,
Missed in their lesson and couldn't spell noise,
Missed in their lesson, oh, was it not sad,
They had to study when others were glad?

Sultry old schoolhouse, benches so high,
Poor little scholars, no wonder you cry!
Were I your teacher, I'd turn you all out
To bask in the sun and frolic about.

When you were rested I'm sure you could say,
That very hard lesson you missed in today,
Spell all the words from n-a-y to noise,
And be just the dearest wee girlie and boys.

—*Jean Ayare.*

In the Garden.

"Here is some pop-corn, dear" I said,
"I'll give you for your own;
    To plant and hoe,
    And watch it grow,
And have it when it's grown."

He took the kernels eagerly,
His little hoe he dropped,
    Then out he burst—
    "Let's pop it first,
So it will come up popped!"

—*Bessie Chandler in St. Nicholas.*

The Straight Path.

The air is for the wing of the sparrow,
  The nest for the robin and wren,
But always the path that is narrow
  And straight for the children of men.

Listen.

If something unkind you hear
About some one you know, my dear,
Do not, I pray you, it repeat
When you *that* "some one" chance to meet;
For such news has a leaden way
Of clouding o'er a sunny day.

But if you something pleasant hear
About some one you know, my dear,
Make haste—to make great haste 'twere well—
To her or him the same to tell;
For such news has a golden way
Of lighting up a cloudy day.
                    —*Harper's Bazar.*

Be noble; and the nobleness that lies
In other men sleeping, but never dead,
Will rise in majesty to meet thine own.
                    —*Lowell.*

The Robin and the Chicken.

A plump little robin flew down from a tree
To hunt for a worm which he happened to see;
A frisky young chicken came scampering by,
And gazed at the robin with wonderful eye.

Said the chick, "What a queer looking chicken is that!
Its wings are so long and its body so fat!"
While the robin remarked, loud enough to be heard,
"Dear me! an exceedingly strange-looking bird!"
"Can you sing?" robin asked, and the chicken said "No!"
But asked in its turn if the robin could crow.
So the bird sought a tree, and the chicken a wall,
And each thought the other knew nothing at all.

—*St. Nicholas.*

Why She Cackled.

"Tut, tut, Biddy Speckle,
Pray hush your loud cackle!
'Tis only an egg you've let drop:
No cause for such flurry,
This flutter and worry;
I dare say 'twill soon be forgot."

"O, dear Mistress Kitty,
Please spare me your pity!
I cackle for joy, don't you see?
This egg I'll be hatching,
And soon he'll be scratching
Fat worms for himself and for me."

—*M. Carey.*

Don't be Caught.

Drop the line with baited hook
In the brook near the nook
Where the fishes like to stay
All the day at their play;
But, like fish, do not be caught,
When with sin's bait you are sought.

The Little Girl's Complaint.

I went with my mama to see
  A little girl today;
I didn't have a bit good time,—
  She don't know how to play.

She wouldn't play make nice dirt pies;
  She's 'fraid of dirt, I s'pose;
She wouldn't climb upon the fence
  Because she'd tear her clothes.

Her mama said we must be good,
  And not make any noise,
'Cause little girls must be polite,
  And not play rude like boys.

She wouldn't let me pick the flowers,—
  They were so pretty, too!
If little girls can't pick them off,
  I wonder why they grew?

I wonder why some ladies think
  It's wrong to run and play,
I don't see how a little girl
  Can keep from noise all day.

My mama says I must not say
  That lady isn't good;
And mama knows what's best—but then
  I only wish I could.
          —*Mrs. Sarah E. Eastman.*

Stick to the truth my little friend,
Begin in youth, and in the end
  You'll find it always pays.

The Frog and the Rat.

A frog and a rat were out traveling one day,
"Kind sir," said the rat, "will you tell me, I pray,
Why are all the people so civil to you,
But glare upon me as though death were my due?"
"My friend," said the frog, "now the reason lies here;
The water is cheap, but the grain it is dear.
If you lived on water, on mud, and such stuff,
The people to you would be civil enough."

Speech for a Little Boy.

Here I am most four feet high,
  I'm brimming full of fun,
I dance and whistle, laugh and sing,
  And hop and skip and run.

I suppose I bother big folks some,
  With all my fun and glee,
But then remember gentle folks
  There is some work in me.

Five days each week I go to school,
  I'm very busy there,
And then of chores and errands too,
  I always have my share.

So please don't scold me when I play,
  Although I make some noise,
It's hard to be so full of fun,
  And still be quiet boys.

I am a little boy you see
  I never spoke before,
But if you'll listen to me now
  I'll tell you something more.

I'll tell you what I mean to be,
   When I am grown a man,
I'll keep the store where letters come,
   I'll be the post-office man.
                    —*F. Louese Walworth*

The Little Digger.

"Whither bound my little lad,
   With spade upon your back?"
"It does not much concern you, sir,
   So please get off my track."

"For what do you intend to dig,
   And where, my little friend?"
"For the pot of gold, sir,
   That at the rainbow's end."
                    —*F. H. Stauffer.*

Poor Dolly.

O, baby, my beautiful baby!
   My own little, dear little Sue!
It is dreadful, just perfectly dreadful,
   To think what has happened to you!
I could cry; but I'm really ashamed to,
   Since you haven't cried—not a wink;
But I know in my heart, precious baby,
   What very sad thoughts you must think.

I'm afraid you'll never believe me,
   But I truly did not mean to fall
And break your poor arm, dear, and hurt you,
   And scratch your sweet rose-cheeks, and all.
I've torn a big hole in my stocking,
   And got a deep scratch in my arm;
But I don't care for anything, dolly,
   Except that I've done you such harm.

Oh, dear! it has spoiled all your beauty,
    And you were so handsome before!
I'm afraid—please excuse me, my darling—
    You'll be "Queen of Beauty" no more.
But oh, I shall love my poor baby
    Far better than ever, I know,
If she weren't most an angel, she never
    Would lie here and smile at me so.
                    —*Mary D. Brine.*

Good Morning.

Good morning, Good morning!
    A new day is here;
Good morning to teacher,
    And school-mates so dear!

I have something to tell you,
    A plan you can try,
How to be very good,
    As the hours pass by.

A plan that will work,
    In the East or the West,
For child or for man;
    This is it—"Do your best."
                    —*E. J. Wallace.*

What Little Boys Can Do.

(For six little boys.)

All—

You think we don't amount to much,
    And call us *horrid boys,*
But we'll prove to you, beyond a doubt,
    We can do more than make a noise.

10

First boy with medal.
> Although I'm but a little lad,
> The medal from my class I've had.

Second boy with bat and ball.
> And I can play at bat and ball
> As well as most boys twice as tall.

Third boy with book and slate.
> I can read and write and spell,
> And always learn my lessons well.

Fourth boy with top and marbles.
> I can spin a top, play marbles too,
> I think I'm getting smart, don't you?

Fifth boy with toy hatchet.
> I run of errands and chop the wood,
> Don't you think that's pretty good?

Sixth boy with kite.
> And I, kind friends, can fly a kite,
> Although I'm such a little mite.

All.
> Although we're only *small boys now*
> Some day we'll be *big men,**
> You'll be proud of us, sure,
> For time will have improved us then.

*All raise right hand above the head.
—*Emily J. Bresee.*

March.

O, March that blusters, and March that blows,
What color under your footsteps glows!
Beauty you summon from winter snows,
And you are the pathway that leads to the rose.

The Happy Days of Summer.

Oh! the happy days of summer,
  When hard lessons are no more,
When the school bells are all silent,
  Tightly closed the school-house door!

When the roses are the thickest,
  Comes vacation's happy hours,
When the sunshine is the brightest,
  Roam the children mid the flowers.

Flo's Letter.

Dear God:

  The baby you brought us
  Is aw-ful nice and sweet,
  But 'cause you for-got his toof-ies,
  The poor little thing can't eat.
  That's why I'm writing this letter,
  A purpose to let you know;
  Please come and finish the baby,
  That's all; From Little Flo.

Vacation.

I have closed my book and hidden my slate,
And thrown my satchel over the gate.
My school is out for a season of rest,
And now for the fields which I love the best.

  Be kind in all you say and do,
  That others may be kind to you.

Shelling Beans.

Such a little woman,
　Gravely shelling beans,
Kitty looks as she would say,
　"Tell me what it means!"

Busy little fingers,
　Eyes of sweetest blue;
"Don't you bother, kitty,
　I have work to do.

"You may sit and watch me
　While I'm shelling beans;
I am helping mother,
　That is what it means."
　　　　　　　—*Lucy R. Fleming.*

Bee-like.

Be like the bee! let every day
Be spent in work or healthful play.
Your mind's a hive in which to store
What you will need when youth is o'er.

The Doll Show.

(Little girl sitting in chair, with seven dolls arranged on a table and chairs with flowers in the background.)

　This is my oldest dolly, you know,
　That grandma gave me a long time ago,
　When I was only a very small girl,
　She was the grandma that named me Pearl.

　I had that one in the blue suit
　Because I was good not to cry for fruit
　Once when I was sick; and I had the next
　Because I was good to remember the text.

That one with the parasol, over there,
Uncle John bought at the Ladies' Fair;
And here are my twins, and both of these
Santa Claus hung on the Christmas trees.

And this is my beauty, she came from France;
She has springs in her feet, and knows how to dance;
And some in her head, so she laughs and cries,
And shuts up and opens her pretty black eyes.

But I don't love her any more than the rest,
I believe I love my old doll the best;
We've been together so long, you see,
I know all about her, she knows all about me.
                              —*M. E. N. Hathaway.*

The Nervous Dollie.

O! Fred, you noisy fellow!
    Stop that racket with your drum!
My dollie's got a headache,
    And her nerves are all unstrung!
                              —*Frank H. Stauffer.*

Hearts-ease

And pansies too are hearts-ease,
    Then like the flowers be,
To thy friends give happiness,
    And "*Hearts-ease*" they'll call thee.

I must, every day,
Be sure that all I say
Is pure and true.

Harry's Mistake.

Grandma was nodding, I rather think;
Harry was sly, and quick as a wink,
He climed on the back of her great arm-chair
And nestled himself very snugly there.
Grandma's dark locks were mingled with white
And quick this little fact came to his sight;
A sharp twinge soon she felt at her hair,
And awoke with a start to find Harry there.
"Why, what are you doing, my child?" she said,
He answered, "I'm pulling a basting thread!"
                    —*Teachers' Institute.*

Little by Little.

Little by little, a small boy said,
And each day the "little" he stored in his head.
Little by little in wisdom he grew,
Learning each day a little that's new,
Till at last the world, in amazement cries
How great is the man,—how wondrous wise.
                    —*From Our Little People.*

Confidential.

O yes it was lovely down there at Cape May,
And I s'posed I should never be tired of play;
And Auntie was sweet as an auntie could be;
But some one was homesick,—you s'pose it was me?

Such elegant ladies and beautiful girls
All asking for kisses and praising my curls;
But no precious papa to hug me, and say,
"Has dear little Kitty been good all the day?"

And mama, O dear, when they turned out the light,
And no blessed mama to kiss me good-night,
Cuddled down in the pillow, with no one to see,
Was a little girl crying—you guess it was me?
—*Emily Huntington Miller.*

The Doll's Mission.

Yes, Fido ate Annabel's head off;
  I really suppose she is dead;
And Dora has swallowed her eyeballs;
  And Claire has a crack in her head.

But Eva has gone on a mission,
  A regular mission—not fun;
She lives at the hospital yonder,
  And wears a gray dress, like a nun.

As soon as I heard of the children,
  The poor little sick ones, you know,
With nothing at all to amuse them,
  I knew 'twas her duty to go.

I loved her the best of my dollies;
  Her eyes were the loveliest blue;
But doing your duty, most always,
  Means something you'd rather not do.

And when I remember the children,
  So tired, and lonesome, and sad,
If I had a houseful of dollies,
  I'd give them the best that I had.
    —*Emily Huntington Miller.*

Attempt the end, and never stand to doubt;
Nothing's so hard, but search will find it out.
    —*Longfellow.*

The War.

Two little chaps with paper caps,
  Flag flying and drum beating,
A charge across the meadow made
  Where flocks of geese were eating.

The geese at this set up a hiss,
  The soldier chaps sought cover,
And out of breath and badly scar'd—
  The cruel war was over,

Ruth Shows the Baby.

Want to see our baby?
  Then walk on your toes,
Boots will hurt a baby,
  Every body knows.

Lift the blanket careful,
  Now, what do you think?
That's a *real* baby,
  Soft and warm and pink.

Just look at her fingers
  Cuddled up so sweet,
But the very best things
  Are her little feet.

Now, I'll tell you something
  Very, very queer—
God forgot to name her
  'Fore He sent her here.

He left that to mama,
  Mama did to me,
So I'm thinking, thinking
  What the name shall be.

No! you shall not name her,
　And she shan't be sold;
She is worth a hundred
　Million pounds of gold.

We don't want your money,
　Not a single bit;
Rather have our baby
　Than the whole of it.

Guess you'd better put her
　Into grandma's lap,
And go way and leave her,
　Baby needs a nap.
　　　　　—Luthera Whitney.

The Timid Doll.

Where can my naughty mother be?
　She's left me quite alone,
And I can't turn my china head
　To see where she has gone.

Oh dear! big dogs will gobble me,
　Great feet will crush me, quite;
I think I'm rolling backward too;
　Oh, I shall die of fright.

Walking in Papa's Footsteps.

'Twas a Sabbath morning bright and fair;
But cold and crispy was the winter air,
For all night long the crystal snow
Had fallen and drifted to and fro;
Till hill and valley seemed to be
Foam-capped billows of a frozen sea.

A holy stillness was everywhere;
And nature herself had knelt in prayer.
No sound of labor from the ice-bound mill,
Even the brook was muffled and still;
No buzz of bee, nor song of bird,
Not even the chirp of a cricket was heard.

The farmer had said at breakfast time,
Before the bells began to chime;
"I only can go to church today,
The snow is too deep for horse and sleigh;
The road-side fences are hidden from view;
I will cross meadow and wood-land, too."

Now sturdy Ralph, but seven years old,
Had never a fear of snow or cold;
He felt himself to be a man.
"If papa can go, I'm sure I can,"
He said to himself, "his tracks I see—
He has plainly marked the way for me."

He reached the church. In the family pew
He quietly sat. When meeting was through
The pastor came, laid his hand on his head,
"How did you get here, my boy?" he said.
"O, it was very easy to find the way—
I walked in papa's footsteps today."

"In papa's footsteps!" said the man of prayer,
"Listen, my friends, take heed, beware!
The children all are following today
In the paths we make, and if they stray
The fault is ours. Take this thought home
And make straight paths in the days to come."

—*American Kindergarten Magazine, Emily D. Elton.*

Ten Little Fingers.

Ten little fingers dimpled and fat
　Now tell us what they can do,
Why they every one of them worked a mat,
　And some of them know how to sew;
And these three here are learning to write—
　That's why they are inky you know.

Ten little fingers, eager and brown
　Whole mornings they live in the sun,
The thimble finger with all the rest
　Once the mud pie season's begun.
And grandma laughs and says, "Ah me
　Little fingers will have their fun."

Ten little fingers, rosy and still
　About mother's neck so tight,
While softly she rocks to the land of dreams
　A sleepy girl in white.
Another busy day is gone by,
　O ten little fingers, good-night.

———

Kind friends, don't think that I'm too small
To stand up here before you all,
　And fill a place like this;
But, bear in mind, that I shall
Grow to be a woman, large, and tall;
　And so I throw you all a kiss.

———

The Brook.

" O stay, little brook! why hasten away?
　The banks here are green, the blossoms are gay.
How are you to know what dangers await
　The path you would go? take heed ere too late."
" I fear nothing, child, when duty is clear;
　God's hand shapes my course! good-by to you dear."
　　　　　　　　　　　　　　　—*J. F. S.*

Mistaken.

I've hunted and I've hunted till my arms and fingers ache;
I'm sure that papa must have made a very queer mistake;
There's nothing here but great big leaves as far as I can tell,
All covered up with dreadful words too hard to speak or spell,
I thought perhaps I'd find my cart I lost so long ago,
Or my quarter, or some marbles, or a dozen knives or so,
But it isn't any use to try, I think I'd better stop,
For I haven't found a single thing, not even my new top,
Yet papa *surely* said: "Now, boys, the dictionary mind,
Is the proper place to look for anything you want to find."

The Fairy Artist.

O there is a little artist,
Who paints in the cold night hours;
Pictures for wee, wee children
Of wondrous trees and flowers.

Pictures of snow-white mountains,
Touching the snow-white sky;
Pictures of distant oceans,
Where pigmy ships sail by.

The moon is the lamp he paints by,
His canvas the window pane;
His brush is the frozen snow-flake,
Jack Frost is the artist's name.

Bessie's Treasures.

I've written all my treasures down,
    I have such lots and lots of things;
A kitten and a little dog,
    A bird that sings;

More picture-books than I can count,
  And dolls—oh, twenty-five, I guess,
Of china, paper, wood, and wax—
  Such fun to dress;
A trunk just full of other toys,
  A lovely ruby ring to wear,
A sewing basket all my own,
  A little chair;
A writing desk—I guess that's all,
  I cannot think of any other,
Except—I really did forget
  My baby brother!

Kittie's Pie.

She caught her apron full of snow,
  This little girl so spry;
And went and packed it on a plate,
  To make a frosted pie.

She put it in the oven then,
  And when she thought 'twas done,
She lifted out an empty plate,
  And that's what made the fun.

To go and do that silly thing,
  She was too old by half.
She said, " I won't tell brother Fred,
  'Twould only make him laugh."

We, while striving, climb the upward way,
And shape by enterprise our inner lives;
But when on some low rest we idly stay,
Our pursose, losing point no longer strives.
                     —*Elliot Stock.*

Ruby's Politeness.

As Ruby's busy little feet
  Were constant patter keeping,
They chanced upon poor puss to step,
  While she lay calmly sleeping.

Then suddenly the laughing face
  Was changed to one of pity,
While anxiously the baby voice
  Cried, " Please *excoose* me, Kitty! "
             —Edith J. Stoddard.

My Ship.

Now, little ship, go out to sea,
And bring good fortune back to me;
But don't like "papa's ship," I pray,
Be gone for ever and a day.

He's always saying what he'll do,
  When *his* ship comes to land;
But somehow it has never come,
  Why, I don't understand.

A single bad habit will mar an otherwise faultless character,
as an ink spot spoileth the pure white page.
             —H. Ballou.

The Sweet-Grass House.

Two little mice went out one day
  Among the scented clover;
They wandered up and down the lane,
  They roamed the meadow over.
"Oh, deary me! " said Mrs. Mouse,
" I wish I had a little house!"

Said Mr. Mouse, "I know a place
  Where nice sweet grass is growing;
Where corn-flowers blue and butter-cups
  And poppies red are blowing."
"Oh, deary me!" said Mrs. Mouse,
  "We'll build us there a house."

So, of some sweet and tender grass,
  They built their house together;
And had a happy time, through all
  ·The pleasant summer weather.
"Oh, deary me!" said Mrs. Mouse,
  "Who ever had so nice a house?"
            —*Mrs. S. J. Brigham.*

Mother's Face.

Three little boys talked together,
  One sunny, summer day,
And I leaned out of the window
  To hear what they had to say.

"The prettiest thing I ever saw,"
  One of the little boys said,
"Was a bird in grandpa's garden,
  All black and white and red."

"The prettiest thing I ever saw,"
  Said the second little lad,
"Was a pony at the circus—
  I wanted him awful bad."

"I think," said the third little fellow,
  With a grave and gentle grace,
"That the prettiest thing in all the world
  Is just my mother's face."

A Patient.

Toast the bread and steep the tea;
Make it dainty as can be;
Spread a napkin on a tray
Some one's very sick today.

There she lies quite pale and still
Poor, some one is very ill;
Wonder how she came to be
Sick enough for toast and tea?

What do you s'pose that you would do
With the saw-dust out of you?
Do you think that *you* could be
Brought to life with toast and tea?

Better be small and shine than great and cast a shadow.

Rev. Theron Brown.

Mud-pies.

With a little water mix a little clay;
Stir it with a crooked stick half the day;
Sweeten it with sand; put in some biscuit crumbs;
White stones for citron, and black stones for plums,
Take it up carefully roll it on a board,
Then you have the best pie money can afford,
Put it on a flat stone, set it in the sun;
There let it bake till the mud-pie is done.

No Drones.

Pull away cheerily, work with a will;
Let not a drone-bee live in the hive;
The world driveth on like a busy old mill,
And each with a web doth busily thrive.

By-and-By.

There's a little mischief-making
  Elfin, who is ever nigh,
Thwarting every undertaking;
  And his name is,—By-and-by.

What we ought to do this minute
  "Will be better done," he'll cry,
"If tomorrow we begin it,"
  "Put it off ," says By-and-by.

Those who heed the treacherous wooing
  Will his faithless guidance rue;
What we always put off doing,
  Clearly we shall never do.

We shall reach what we endeavor,
  If on "*Now*" we more rely
But unto the realms of "Never,"
  Leads the pilot, By-and by.

Bread-Making.

Now you place it in the bread bowl,
  A smooth and nice dough-ball,
Last a towel and a cover,
  And at night that's all.
But when morning calls the sleeper
  From her little bed,
She can make our breakfast biscuit
  From that batch of bread.

Today.

Don't tell me of to-morrow,
  Give me the boy who'll say
That when a good deed's to be done,
  "Let's do the deed today."

12

The Bird.

"Come little bird, I have waited some time,
Light on my hand and I'll give you a dime,
I have a cage that will keep you warm,
Free from danger, and safe from harm."

"No, little lady, we cannot do that,
Not for a dime, or a brand new hat,
We are so happy and wild and free,
Chee-dee-dee! Chee-dee-dee!"

"Fly, pretty bird, fly down, and take
Just a crumb of my Christmas cake;
Santa Claus brought it to me, you know,
Over the snow, Over the snow."

"Yes we know of your home so rare,
And stockings hung in the firelight there;
We peeped through the window blinds to see,
Chee-dee-dee! Chee-dee-dee!"

We were on the button-wood tree,
Closer than you thought us to be;
Soon you may have us in to tea,
Chee-dee-dee! Chee-dee-dee!

Fish.

Our lesson is fish, and in every wish,
We would like to meet our teacher's wish,
But many men have many minds,
There are many fishes of many kinds;
So we only learn to boil and bake,
To broil and fry and make a fish cake,
And trust this knowledge will carry us through
When other fishes we have to do.

Johnny's Garden.

Johnny had a garden plot,
  And set it all in order,
But let it run to grass and weeds,
  Which covered bed and border.

Two stalking sun-flowers reared their head,
  So firmly were they rooted,
And Johnny as he looked at them,
  Was anything but suited.

Two children small, looked up and said,
  " Oh, Mister, beg your pardon!
Or, if you will not answer that,
  Say, sonny, where's your garden? "

" What d'ye call those two large flowers?
  An' what'll ye take, and sell 'em?
You'd better put a ladder up,
  So folks our size can smell 'em.

" We heard old Mrs. Grubber say,
  ' That spot ye needn't covet;
He'd better turn it into hay,
  Or make a grass-plot of it.' "

But Johnny never answered back,
  But went and dug it over,
And soon again, his sprouting seeds,
  He plainly could discover.

He said, " I'll have a garden yet,
  And make a little money;
I never liked those Podger twins—
  They try to be so funny."
          —From Bright Jewels.

Snow Balls.

Look, boys, here's plenty of snow,
Just right to make balls I know!
   So come every one,
    We'll have lots of fun,
And see how far we can throw.

Bad I Can't.

Leave our school-room,
  Bad I can't;
Leave it now forever!
We will try, and try again,
And listen to you *never*.

Leave us, leave us,
  Bad I can't;
You have naughty brothers—
Will, and shall, and won't and sha'n't,
And too many others.

Good-by, good-by,
  Bad I can't;
Shut the door behind you;
In this school-room never more
Shall our teacher find you.

            —*Our Little Ones.*

The Birds' Meeting.

The blust'ry wind had called them all;
The birds arrived, the large, the small.
The owl, of course, was chosen judge;
He stared around, but did'nt budge.

The robins, jays, and meadowlarks
Got up to make a few remarks;
They said the time had come to go,
Red leaves and gold flew to and fro.

The sparrows then grew spitefull quite,
They thought it much too soon for flight;
But bluebirds longed for bluer skies,
And wrens thought this was very wise.

The blackbirds said their time was up;
The berries gone, where should they sup?
The catbirds said they quite agreed,
'Twas time the warning they should heed.

The owl this question put: "Say 'Ay,'
Those who intend away to fly!"
All but the sparrows vote to go;
These cheep a most decided "No!"

" 'Tis carried," said the owl; "adieu!"
The birds cry, "Now for skies more blue,"
"Go!" chirped the sparrows, "why this fuss?
Our home is good enough for us!"

—*George Cooper.*

Three Little Friends.

Under the tree, under the tree,
Contented and happy sit little friends three.
The sunbeams so gay make a beautiful day
For our little girlies to frolic away.

Up in the tree, up in the tree,
The birdies are hiding as snug as can be;
The little black cat is too lazy and fat
And too busy purring to care about that.

—*M. D. Brine.*

Dandelions.

"I think," said mother Golden-Head
    To all her children dear,—
"I think we'd better be astir,
    And see how things appear."

Then forth she led them one by one,
    Through fields and meadows sweet;
A gayer troop of Golden-Heads
    'Tis rare for one to meet.

"Good morning, Mistress Golden-Head,"
    Said modest Daisy White;
"It seems to me I never saw
    You look so fresh and bright.

"Pray tell me where you've been to find
    Such lovely shining hair;
There's nothing in these parts, I know,
    That can at all compare."

"I think I've only been asleep,
    Yes, fast asleep," she said;
"And while I slept the fairies poured
    Gold-dust upon my head."
                —*Elizabeth A. Davis.*

By doing only can we know,
What it is we have to do.

The Moon is a Lady.

The moon, the moon, the silver moon!
    The moon is a lady fair;
She has a great, round, smiling face,
    And long, bright, shining hair.

I think way up amid the clouds
   She lives in a palace bright;
She keeps the curtains drawn all day,
   And opens them at night.

Awhile she at her casement sits,
   And spins with her fingers spry
A long white veil of moonbeams bright
   To float upon the sky.

And then behind her flying steeds
   She rides in her golden car
O'er daisy fields where every flower
   Is just a twinkling star.
            —Nellie M. Garabrant.

Little Mishap.

Little Mishap,
On grandmother's lap,
Is telling a wonderful story,
About an odd dame
Of Mother Goose fame,
Known sometimes as "Old Mother Morey."

"She killed a fat calf!"
"Now, grandma that's half,"
"Yes, child, and where did she throw it?"
"Why over the wall,"
"Yes, dear, and that's all."
"O, grandma! how came *you* to know it?"
            —Our Little Ones.

So let your faults be what they may,
To own them is the better way.

Six Years Old.

(Little girl talking to a doll in the chair.)

What do you think, doll Rosa?
Look sharp at me, and say!
What do you think has happened?
　I'm six years old today.
Yes, that is why my dear mama
Has dressed you up so gay,
And brought you here to visit me—
　I'm six years old today!

You see how fast I'm growing?
Oh, I forgot, you know,
That you had only met me
　An hour or two ago!
I've grown a year since yesterday!
My papa told me so.
I'm sure I didn't feel so tall
　A day or two ago!

And don't you think, doll Rosa,
I'm 'most too old to play?
I really feel quite busy,
　Because I'm six today.
1 guess I'll help mama awhile!
I wonder what she'll say.
And after that we'll celebrate!
　Because I'm six today.
　　　　　　　　　—*Uncle Felix.*

Nan and her Kitten.

Poor little black Topsy, I'm sorry to say,
Is feeling too badly to work or to play.
So Nan said, " Now, Topsy, the day is so fair,
I think you'd feel better dear out in the air.

And when you go in you shall have catnip tea,
I'm sure that will make you as well as can be.
Now don't you think, Kitty, 'twill be good for you?
But poor little Topsy could only say, " Mew."

Dolly's Lesson.

(Little girl in cap and spectacles; an open book in her left hand, showing
A, B, C; in her right a pointer; while before her is a doll placed in a chair.)

Come, Dolly, will you learn to read?
  I have a pretty book;
Nay, turn this way, you must indeed!
  Fie! there's a sulky look.

Here is a pretty picture, see,
  An apple, and great A,
How stupid you will ever be,
  If you do naught but play!

Come; A, B, C, an easy task,
  What anyone can do,
I will do anything you ask,
  For dearly I love you.

Now, how I'm vexed; you are so dull!
  You have not learnt it half;
You will grow up a downright dunce,
  And make all people laugh.
          —*From Happy Times.*

Bunny and Birdie.

"Go 'way, go 'way!" said birdie,
  "You long-tailed frisky thing,
You have no right to be here,
  You don't know how to sing."

13

"Chip, chip!" said little bunny;
  "Please, ma'am, I'll go away;
I didn't touch your eggs, ma'am,
  I only came to play."

"Well, hurry up," said birdie;
  "My eggs will all get cold,
You'd better take yourself off,
  Or else you'll hear me scold."

"Phit, phit!" said little bunny,
  "I'm going right away,"
And down the tree he hurried,
  "Good-day," he said, "good-day."

The Chickadee-dee.

Little darling of the snow,
Careless how the winds may blow,
Happy as a bird can be,
Singing, oh, so cheerily,
Chickadee-dee! Chickadee-dee!

When the skies are cold and gray,
When he trills his happiest lay,
Through the clouds he seemed to see
Hidden things to you and me.
Chickadee-dee! Chickadee-dee!

Very likely little birds
Have their thoughts too deep for words,
But we know, and all agree,
That the world would dreary be
Without birds, dear chickadee!
                    —*Elizabeth A. Davis.*

Telephoning.

(Little girl, seated on chair, with a large spool in her hand, to which a string is attached. A dolly, with cloth tied around her head, a cup with spoon near her. An older girl, representing mama, is seated at a table farther away sewing—She uses a spool as receiver and transmitter.)

Minnie Midget puts the spool to her ear, calls:
"Hello, Central! don't you hear?
Give me Forty—twenty-four!
Mama's house? halloo! halloo!
That you, mama? Stay right there!
I've a message all for you."

Mama.
"All right, baby, I can hear;
What would Midget like to say?"

Midget.
"Mama, are you truly, true,
Hearing every single thing,—
What I think, and say, and sing,—
As if I were close to you?"

Mama.
"Yes, I hear, my little one,
Every word so plain and clear
I might almost think you here,
Speaking with no telephone!"

Midget.
"Well, you please to tell the doctor
Dolly has the stomach-ache;
Wants some pepper-mints to take.
All-the day I've sat and watched her,
And please, mama, I love you!"

Mama.
"All right, baby, here is one,
Doctor sends through telephone,
And a kiss for Midget, too."

Midget.

"Thank you, mama; now I'll try
To get Seventy-One-Two-Nine,—
Aunty's house,—to talk to mine;
All through, mama dear! Good by."
                    —*From Little Ones, G. S. Burleigh.*

Trifles.

A little bit of patience often makes the sunshine come,
And a little bit of love makes a very happy home.
A little bit of hope makes a rainy day look gay,
And a little bit of charity makes glad a weary way.

Recitation.
(For five little girls.)

The city maiden.

I'm a little city maiden,
    You would know it by my style;
I'm quite unlike those country rustics,
    With their broad and courteous smile.
I shall not soil *my* hands with labor,
    I was born for higher things;
Papa calls me little angel
    And says all I lack is wings.

The country lassie.

I'm a little country lassie,
    I can iron, churn and bake,
Wash the dishes, feed the poultry,
    And make a famous "Johnny cake;"
Ride the horses down to water,
    Drive the cows to pastures green:
I would not change my station,
    For the throne of England's queen.

The little student.

 I'm papa's little student,
  I can cipher, read and spell;
 Draw a map, and bound a country,
  And in mental I excel;
 I shall climb the tree of knowledge,
  To the very top I'll go;
 Then success shall crown my efforts,
  Teacher says, and ain't it so?

The noodle.

 I'm nothing but a noodle,
  Mother told me so today,
 But I really cannot study,
  When the very fields are gay.
 Birds are calling from the tree tops,
  Spring is laughing in the rills;
 You may mope o'er prosy lessons,
  I will be a noodle still.

The darling.

 I am mama's little darling,
  Don't you think I'm fresh and sweet,
 With these flowers at my shoulder.
  And my muslin dress so neat?
 Mama made it just on purpose,
  'Cause I was going to speak to you,
 It is pretty, don't you think so?
  Wish 'twas yours?—I guess you do.

 Clear the track! Quick, turn back!
 Here come the sleds with the boys!
 Rosy cheeks! Funny freaks!
 And never-ceasing noise.

February Rain.

Drip, drip, all day long!
Not a sunbeam, not a song!
Creeping fog for breezes gay,
And for sky a blanket gray!
Patter, patter on the pane
Dreary February rain!
Yet, dear child, such days must be,
Or, 'twere ill for thee and me:
Hill and forest, vale and plane,
Love this February rain.
'Neath these dreary, dripping skies,
They are storing up supplies
In recesses cool and sweet,
For the time of summer heat.
They will give it out again,
Dew and fog, and mist and rain,
For broad fields of waving grain,
And fair flowers that gem the plain.
Mountain springs must drink their fill,
Feed each tiny trickling rill;
And the rill a river grow,
Where great ships may come and go;
And the earth distribute food
To the evil and the good.
When the daisies star the field,
And the months their bounty yield
Of ripe fruits, bethink thee then
Of the ways of God to men—
How His tender, constant care
Just and unjust equal share,
As He waters hill and plain
With the treasures of his rain.

—E. E. C. Glasier.

Hunting Woodchucks.

Frank: Hello, hello! Is that you Joe?
What are you doing, I'd like to know?

Joe: Hunting woodchucks; don't you see,
They're just as thick as they can be.

Frank: Well, I'm glad a bag I brought;
Say, how many have you caught?

Joe: How many? Oh, I shall have four,
When I get this one and three more.
—*Kindergarten Magazine.*

Exercise for Six Little Boys.

Robbie: Tomorrow will be Saturday,
No school the livelong day!
No lessons we will have to learn,
Nothing to do but play!
Suppose we spend a little while
Talking about the fun
We mean to have on Saturday,
When all our work is done.
Let each one tell what he will do
To spend a pleasant day,
If he is going to visit friends,
Or stay at home and play.
Now Tommy, I'll begin with you;
Tell me what you are going to do.

Tommy: I plan so much for Saturday,
It's hard now to decide;
But still, to you, I will confess
It always is my pride
To have my many pockets lined

With marbles by the score;
And so tomorrow I will try
If I can win some more.

Robbie: And do you think that you will win?

Tommy: At any rate, I'll try,
And just what my success may be
I'll tell you by and by.

Robbie: Indeed, I hope you'll meet success,
And have a jolly game;
Now, Arnold, we will hear from you,
Are you to do the same?

Arnold: Yes, I will join in Tommy's game,
I promised so today,
We always play together, he
But lives two doors away.
Tommy, I see, is going to win,
But I don't think it's so;
You cannot tell who wins a game,
Until it's played—you know.

Robbie: I wish you both a pleasant game
And come out square when done.
Now, Leo, it is your turn next,
Are you to have some fun?

Leo: Oh! I am going to see my aunt,
She lives some miles away,
And she has often asked me out
To make a little stay.
And so tomorrow morning, I
The early train will take,
I'll see the great long line of cars,
And hear the noise they make.
The engine it will dash along,

And scream in wildest glee,
Then at the station it will stop
And Aunt will welcome me.
All day I'll run the pastures through
Where cattle graze at ease;
I'll watch the birds that build their nests
Upon the highest trees;
I'll climb upon the old hay-mow
And laugh and shout and sing;
And oh! I'll have such jolly fun
Upon the old barn swing.

Robbie: Indeed you'll have a splendid time,
Wish I were going too!
But, Albert, it is your turn now,
We want to hear from you.

Albert: Oh! I have joined a base ball club,
Tomorrow we all play;
Why don't you come and see the game,
If it's a pleasant day?
We've got the best ball ever made,
And two fine, brand new bats;
And all the club are dressed alike,
In base ball suits and hats;
We made the very finest score,
With ease, the other day;
I wish, tomorrow, all would come
And see how well we play.

Robbie: Well, if I've time, I will go down;
I much like bat and ball,
Now, Willie, what have you to say?
The very last of all.

Willie: I am quite glad to hear you talk
About your many plays,

14

But my mama has been quite sick
For very many days;
And so tomorrow I can't play,
I'll have some work to do,
My little brother I must mind
And keep him quiet too.
He is the greatest little rogue
To throw his toys about;
And then I have to pick them up,
Or he will scream and shout.
And then there are some errands, too,
Mama says must be done;
But doing just such work as this
The best boys call but fun.
But when mama has grown quite well,
Then I can with you play
At marbles, top, and bat, and ball,
And frolic all the day.

Robbie: I'm sorry your mama is sick,
But work's as good as play,
And I'm sure that you will spend
Of all, the happiest day.
—*Jane E. Gormley, in American Teacher.*

Our Pets.

All:

What pretty little creatures
  Surround us everywhere,
Both in the fields and wild woods
  And flying through the air.
We hear sweet voices calling
  Wherever we may roam,
But best we love the voices
  Of little pets at home.

First Child:

> I have a little kitty,
>   As cunning as can be,
> And ev'ry night and morning,
>   She plays along with me.
> She paws my ball of worsted
>   And climbs upon my chair;
> This playful little kitten
>   Makes mischief everywhere.

Second Child:

> I have a little doggie,
>   As nimble as can be;
> He is the swiftest racer
>   That ever you did see.
>   Both sticks and stones he chases
> All up and down the street.
>   You'd laugh to see my doggie
> Beg for a piece of meat!

Third Child:

> I have a little rabbit,
>   His fur is soft as down,
> His ears are long and pointed,
>   His pretty eyes are brown.
> I gather leaves and grasses,
>   Such things he likes to eat,
> Then standing on his hind legs,
>   He thanks me for the treat.

Fourth Child:

> I have a pet Canary,
>   His music is so sweet!
> I give him plenty bread crumbs,
>   And worms and seeds to eat.
> His cage hangs in the window,
>   And in the warm sunlight;
> He chirps and sings so happy
>   From early morn till night.

Fifth Child:

My little lamb is snow-white;
  He runs and skips and plays,
And nibbles grass and flowers
  On pleasant summer days.
His wool so soft and fleecy,
  With us he'll kindly share,
To make us pretty dresses
  In winter time to wear.

Sixth Child:

I have a funny parrot,
  That talks as well as you,
He whistles, oh, so loudly,
  And laughs and chatters too!
I know you'd like to see him;
  It's such a funny thing
To watch him swinging gaily
  Upon his painted ring.

All:

These are the pretty creatures
  That fill us with delight;
That wake us in the morning
  Before the coming light.
They help to make the sunshine
  We always find in play;
So, pretty little creatures,
  We sing of you today.
           —*Jane E. Gormley.*

Love.

Little children, love each other.
  Show true love to great and small;
Love your father and your mother,
  And love God the most of all.

Cheery Hearts.

Oh, what a lot of pleasure
Sweet, smiling faces bring,
And what a lot of music in pleasant voices ring!
The skies may meet in sadness,
The blustering winds may blow,
But if our hearts are cheery, there's
Sunshine where we go.
     —*Little Poems for Little Children.*

The Boys We Need.

Here's to the boy who's not afraid
 To do his share of work;
Who never is by toil dismayed,
 And never tries to shirk.

The boy whose heart is brave to meet
 All lions in the way;
Who's not discouraged by defeat,
 But tries another day.

The boy who always means to do
 The very best he can;
Who always keeps the right in view,
 And aims to be a man.

Such boys as these will grow to be
 The men whose hands will guide
The future of our land; and we
 Shall speak there names with pride.

All honor to the boy who is
 A man at heart, I say;
Whose legend on his shield is this,
 "Right always wins the day."

What to Feed the Rabbits.

Tell me quickly, someone;
  For I want to know,
What to feed a rabbit
  That will make him grow.

Bread and cheese and honey
  Is what they give to me;
But bread and cheese and honey
  He won't eat, you see.

Three Fishers.

Three little fishermen, down by the bay,
Went on a voyage one sunshiny day;
Dick had the bait in a pink china dish,
Ted had a basket, to bring home the fish,
And Tommy, the captain, went marching along
With a gold-headed rod on his shoulder so strong.

Three little fishermen, out on the bay,
Laughing and shouting went sailing away,
Sailing away with the wind and the tide,
And the little waves danced as they ran by the side;
But the worms wriggled out of the pink china dish,
And the gold-headed rod only frightened the fish.

Three little fishermen, out on the bay,
Weeping and wailing, went drifting away,
Till a grimy old oysterman brought them to land,
And set them down safe in a row on the sand;
But the gold-headed rod, and the pink china dish,
And the big willow basket were left for the fish.
  —*Emily Huntington Miller, in Our Little Ones.*

The Road to School.

In winter when it freezes,
  In winter when it snows,
The road to school seems long and drear,
  O'er which the school boy goes.

But when the pleasant summer comes,
  With birds and fruit and flowers,
The road to school, how short it is!
  And short the sunny hours!

But to the boy who loves to learn,
  And wisdom strives to gain,
The road to school is always short.
  In sunshine, snow or rain.
                —L. A. B. C.

Baby's Dream.

What do you think our baby dreamed
Asleep in his little bed?
He dreamed a little angel came,
And held a star like a golden flame
Which he waved o'er baby's head;
And since, when baby sees a star,
He wonders where the angels are.

The Better Way.

'Tis better to laugh than to cry, dear,
  A proverb you'll grant me is true,
'Tis best to forget to be sad, dear,
  The hearts-ease is better than rue.

'Tis best to be glad for what is, dear,
  Than to sigh for the things which are not,
'Tis braver to reckon the joys, dear,
  Than the troubles that fall to your lot.

'Tis more to be good than great, dear,
  To be happy is better than wise,
You will find if you smile at the world, dear,
  The world will smile back in your eyes.
                              —*H. L. Towne.*

The Dandelion.

Bright little dandelion,
  Downy yellow face,
Peeping up among the grass
  With such gentle grace;
Minding not the April wind
  Blowing rude and cold,
Brave little dandelion,
  With a heart of gold!

Meek little dandelion,
  Changing into curls
At the magic touch of these
  Merry boys and girls!
When they pinch thy dainty throat,
  Strip thy dress of green,
On thy soft and gentle face
  Not a cloud is seen!

Poor little dandelion,
  All gone to seed,
Scattered roughly by the winds,
  Like a common weed!
Thou hast lived thy little life,
  Smiling every day;
Who could do a better thing
  In a better way?

Pine Needles.

If mother nature patches
 The leaves of trees and vines,
I'm sure she does her darning
 With needles of the pines!
They are so long and slender;
 And sometimes, in full view,
They have their thread of cobwebs,
 And thimbles made of dew!

The Moon and the Stars.

The moon and her children went early one day,
Across the blue sky by the "milky way,"
To visit the sun in his palace of gold,
Of whose wonders the stars had often been told.

Each morning their eyes had been closed in sleep,
So they could never get of the sun a peep,
This jolly old sun who was ages old,
And who lived near the Dawn in a house of gold.

The mother moon whispered the night before,.
As she piled up the clouds on the azure floor
And tucked the dear little children up in their beds,
With night-caps of snow on their golden heads,
Tomorrow we'll go by the "milky way."

Kind words are the music of the world.
—F. W. Faber.

God means every man to be happy, be sure,
He sends us no sorrows that have not some cure.
15

Getting Ready.

Gain a little useful knowledge
  Every day, my boy,
Search for secrets that are hidden
  In your tool or toy;
Do not shrink from *when* and *wherefore*,
  How and *which* and *why*—
They are helpers to prepare you
  For the by-and-by.

By-and-by, when to your labor
  You go forth a man,
And the goal you seek seems saying,
  "Gain me, if you can!"
A good acorn holds an oak-tree;
  So success may find
Its beginning in the richness
  Of a well stored mind.

By-and-By.

"By-and-By" is a very bad boy;
  Shun him at once and forever;
For they who travel with "By-and-by,"
  Soon come to the house of "Never."

"I Can't" is a mean little coward;
  A boy that is half of a man:
Set on him a plucky wee terrier
  That the world knows and honors—"I can."

"No use in trying"—nonsense I say,
  Keep trying until you succeed:
But if you should meet "I forgot" by the way,
  He's a cheat and you'd better take heed.

"Don't care" and "No matter," boys, they're a pair,
  And whenever you see the poor dolls,
Say, yes, I do care, and 'twould be *great matter*
  If our lives should be spoilt by such faults.

Our Heroes.

Here's a hand to the boy who has courage
  To do what he knows to be right;
When he falls in the way of temptation
  He has a hard battle to fight.
Who strives against self and his comrades
  Will find a most powerful foe;
All honor to him if he conquers,
  A cheer for the boy who says "No!"

There's many a battle fought daily
  The world knows nothing about;
There's many a brave little soldier
  Whose strength puts a legion to rout.
And he who fights sin single-handed
  Is more of a hero, I say,
Than he who leads soldiers to battle,
  And conquers by arms in the fray.

Be *steadfast* my boy, when you're tempted,
  To *do* what you *know* to be *right*;
Stand *firm* by the colors of manhood,
  And you will o'ercome in the fight.
"The Right" be your battle-cry ever
  In waging the warfare of life;
And God, knowing who are the heroes,
  Will give you the strength for the strife.

Example sheds a genial ray
  Of light that men are apt to borrow;
So first improve *yourself* today
  And then improve *your friends* tomorrow.
            --*Valentine Vousden.*

A Boy's Plea.

They say that boys make all the noise,
  And that the girls are quiet;
If girls were boys I know their joys
  Would only be in riot.

I know we oft, when mud is soft,
  Forget to use the door-mats;
We go "all fours," we slam the doors,
  We use our hats like brick-bats.

Perhaps we may some sunny day,
  Attempt to tease the girls;
To eat their cake, and faces make,
  Or pull their dangling curls.

But then you know, when we do so,
  Its only just in fun,
For when we will, we can be still,
  As almost any one.

But let them say whate'er they may
  About our dreadful noise,
For errands done, some one to run,
  They're glad to find the boys.

Not the Manly Boys.

It isn't the boy who doubles his fists,
  And thrusts them under another's nose,
Baring the sleeves from his rigid wrists,
  Ready to rain vindictive blows;
Whose tongue is ready with jibe and jeer
  To stir up strife whenever he can,
Breathing menace and waking fear,
  Who grows to be a *manly* man.

Off the Line.

The boys stood up in the reading class -
A dozen or so—and each one said,
"That those at the foot should never pass,
Or find it easy to reach the head."

Harry was studious, and so was Jake,
Jim and Robert, and Tom and Jack;
For men of business they meant to make,
And it wouldn't do to be dull or slack.

There wasn't another boy on the line
More anxious than Jimmy to keep his place;
For, to be at head, was very fine,
But to go down foot was a sad disgrace.

But Jim delighted in games of ball,
Polo, tennis, or tame croquet,
And his mind was not on his book at all
When he took his place in his class that day.

'Twas his turn to read, and he started off,
With an attentive air—a vain pretence;
For the boys around him began to cough,
And nudge and chuckle at Jim's expense.

"You've skipped a line," whispered generous Ben
Who often had helped in this way before,
"You've skipped a line," shouted Jim, and then—
Of course the schoolroom was in a roar;

As down to the foot Jim went that day,
He learned a lesson that any dunce
Might have known for we're sure to stray
If we try to be in two places at once.

Room at the Top.

Never you mind the crowd, lad,
  Nor fancy your life won't tell;
The work is done for all that,
  To him who doeth it well.

Fancy the world a hill, lad,
  Look where the millions stop;
You'll find the crowd at the base, lad;
  But there's always room at the top.

Courage, and faith and patience!
  There's space in the old world yet;
You stand a better chance, lad,
  The further along you get.

Keep your eye on the goal, lad,
  Never despair or drop;
Be sure your path leads upwards—
  There's always room at the top.

There is no worse robber than a bad book.

Lullaby.

Wynken, Bynken, and Nod one night
  Sailed off in a wooden shoe—
Sailed on a river of misty light
  Into a sea of dew.
"Where are you going and what do you wish?"
  The old moon asked the three,
"We have come to fish for the herring fish
  That live in this beautiful sea:
Nets of silver and gold have we,"
  Said Wynken, Blynken and Nod.

The old moon laughed and sang a song,
  As they rocked in the wooden shoe,
And the wind that sped them all night long
  Ruffled the waves of dew;
The little stars were the herring fish
  That lived in the beautiful sea—
"Now cast your nets wherever you wish,
  But never afeard are we"
So cried the stars to the fishermen three,
  Wynken, Blynken, and Nod.

All night long their nets they threw
  For the fish in the twinkling foam—
Then down from the sky came the wooden shoe,
  Bringing the fishermen home;
'Twas all so pretty a sail, it seemed
  As if it could not be;
And some folk thought 'twas a dream they dreamed
  Of sailing that beautiful sea—
But I shall name you the fishermen three;
  Wynken, Blynken and Nod.

Wynken and Blynken are two little eyes,
  And Nod is a little head,
And the wooden-shoe that sailed the skies,
  Is a wee one's trundle-bed;
So shut your eyes while mother sings
  Of wonderful sights that be,
And you shall see the beautiful things
  As you rock on the misty sea
Where the old shoe rocked the fishermen three—
  Wynken, Blynken and Nod
                    —*E. F. in Chicago News.*

By doing, only, can we know
  What it is we have to do.

If.

If everything were different,
　　And each the other way,
I wonder what the world would be
　　And where we'd be today.
If men beneath the ocean lived
　　Instead of on the land
And dwelt in sea shell palaces,
　　With floors of shining sand;
If darkness reigned instead of light,
　　If each star closed its eye;
If every bird should cease to sing.
　　If every flower should die;
If butterflies and bumblebees
　　Should visit us no more,
Fair earth should be a desert drear
　　And dark from shore to shore.
If over fleecy clouds we walked,
　　If heaven, like earth, were brown,
If thunder roared beneath our feet,
　　If trees grew upside down;
If elephants were small as mice,
　　If fishes fed on grass,—
But all my *ifs* are foolish thoughts;
　　They'll never come to pass.
　　　　　Lily A. Muldowny—Boston—Aged 13.

All Clean.

Every little birdie I have ever seen,
Washes every morning, keeps himself quite clean.
And my cunning kitty scrubs herself with care;
Then, to be quite tidy, smoothly combs her hair.
All the pretty flowers blooming sweet for you,
In the early morning bathe in purest dew.
So we little children must be clean as they,
Wash our hands and faces, comb our hair each day.

You'll Find It Always Pays.

Be happy! gather on life's road,
  The sweetest flowers you find!
Some pleasures are for you bestowed,
  But choose the proper kind.
How fair a face temptation has,
  How joyous seem her ways;
Look not thereon, but bravely pass--
  You'll find it always pays!

Though here on earth, or there above,
  Be now that heart we prize,
Remember that a mother's love
  Is one that never dies.
So heed the counsel she would give,
  That good attend your days;
And let them guide you while you live:
  You'll find it always pays!

Honor the aged, as you should,
  And give them reverence due;
And "do to others as you would
  That they should do to you!"
A kind word here, a good deed there,
  Like sunshine casts its rays,
And makes the world more pure and fair;
  You'll find it always pays!

Be honest in your dealings all—
  In every word you say:
Then you may never fear to fall,
  Nor shun the light of day.
Stick to the truth, my little friend,
  And hold the word that strays!
Begin in youth, and in the end
  You'll find it always pays!
            —*George Birdseye, in Golden Days.*

16

INDEX.